LEADERSHIP LANDSCAPES

LEADERSHIP LANDSCAPES

Tom Cummings

and

Jim Keen

First published in 2008 by
PALGRAVE MACMILLAN
Houndmills, Basingstoke, Hampshire RG21 6XS and
175 Fifth Avenue, New York, N.Y. 10010
Companies and representatives throughout the world

PALGRAVE MACMILLAN is the global academic imprint of the Palgrave Macmillan division of St. Martin's Press, LLC and of Palgrave Macmillan Ltd. Macmillan® is a registered trademark in the United States, United Kingdom and other countries. Palgrave is a registered trademark in the European Union and other countries.

ISBN-13: 978–0–230–52569–6
ISBN-10: 0–230–52569–5

This book is printed on paper suitable for recycling and made from fully managed and sustained forest sources. Logging, pulping and manufacturing processes are expected to conform to the environmental regulations of the country of origin.

A catalogue record for this book is available from the British Library.

A catalog record for this book is available from the Library of Congress.

10 9 8 7 6 5 4 3 2 1
17 16 15 14 13 12 11 10 09 08

Printed and bound in Great Britain by
Cromwell Press Ltd, Trowbridge, Wiltshire

TABLE OF CONTENTS

PREFACE

This book emerges from a conversation between the authors that commenced nearly 25 years ago in a Harvard Square consulting office when Tom Cummings was assigned to take the lead on a project in which Jim Keen had a continuing role. The project was for the Club of Rome, a transnational group of 100 mostly senior leaders from business, government, academia, and foundations that had been drawn together by the Italian industrialist Aurelio Peccei. From the first, we sensed some common commitments and attitudes. We liked to ask big questions. We were fascinated by the dynamics of innovation and the processes of change, in people, in organizations, and in the world. We shared a pragmatic idealism that compelled us to try to make a real difference in the world through enabling others to do their best work. We were each committed to engaging in reflective practice and inquiry aimed at discovering and developing the best practices to support the leveraging of progressive change. Perhaps most importantly, both of us thrived on getting alongside others and on engaging in collaborative thought and action.

Our work for the Club of Rome focused on an initiative that was cut short by Aurelio Peccei's death, just one month after we joined together to report to him on that work. We also reported to him on a leadership development program that Jim and his wife had designed and implemented for the Governor of New Jersey as a demonstration of participatory and innovative learning as espoused in the report to the Club of Rome, No Limits to Learning.[1] It was in this four-week intensive program that Tom actually received his introduction to teaching.

Our conversation ebbed and flowed through a variety of contexts until the late 1990s when the tide of events brought us to the episode of collaboration that has produced this book. This recent work has taken the form of what we refer to as "conversational partnership," a practice we describe in Chapter 8. At times our conversation has involved coaching, mostly with Tom as client and Jim as coach and advisor. At moments these roles have been reversed. More of the time it has been dialogue, working at an idea, a problem or a design together and through multiple reframings coming up with fresh ideas and concepts to keep us on the cutting edge of our practices. Sometimes it has been hard going, as we grappled with daunting, seemingly intractable challenges. Almost all of the time it has felt mutual, with the two of us in the frame together, making meaning, building concepts and designs.

In this conversation we have drawn on each other's experience and insights to integrate a fresh set of understandings that clarify the practice that Tom has forged in the architecture and delivery of custom designed leadership development initiatives for his corporate clients, as well as his work facilitating and coaching corporate boards and leadership teams. The conversation has also drawn on Jim's previous research (particularly the work with Laurent Daloz, Cheryl Keen, and Sharon Parks that led to their book, *Common Fire*) as well as on his long experience in coaching in the design and evaluation of leadership development programs. The result has been to enrich our collaboration as well as the individual practices in which we are engaged.

Since the first days of this conversation, when both of us lived within easy distance of Harvard Square, our conversations have involved journeys. Tom has lived his professional life in the business world, mostly in Europe, while working at times in the United States. Jim continues to reside in the United States while dividing his time between the two sides of the Atlantic. Our conversational partnership is most generative when we make sure we talk regularly, face to face, and for most of the past ten years our talks have involved one of us in transatlantic travel. Some of our most productive work has emerged as we have journeyed together by car from one European city to another.

The depth and duration of our conversational journey makes it difficult to say that one or the other of us is responsible for this or that idea in this book. The concepts have taken root and come to fruition in the context of conversational partnership. We honor this by speaking at times in the first person plural. At other times, when the narrator appears as "I," the reader can be sure it is one or the other of us, relating something from first hand experience where the "we" voice would feel inappropriate. And we often narrate in the third person as well. The combination of these several narrative perspectives feels right to us and we hope it proves as comfortable to you.

How do we place our ideas among some of the existing ideas on leadership, teams, and organizations? Half a century ago, Peter Drucker was one of the first to trek across the "modern" business landscape. He took us to its very edge and along the way, sign-posted "The Landmarks of Tomorrow" to show us the path of what was to come. In 1957 he proclaimed, as only Peter Drucker could:

We have imperceptibly moved out of the "Modern Age" and into a new, as yet nameless era. Our view of the world has changed; we have acquired a new perception and with it new capacities. There are new frontiers of opportunity, risk and challenge. There is a new spiritual centre to human existence.

Drucker could hardly have known what "new challenges" the world would bring. Yet he knew that the "postmodern world" (his nameless era) would change our perceptions and capacities forever, and together with our new consciousness we would develop the necessary capacities as business leaders to survive. Fifty years on, we now know what some of these capacities and perceptions are, and at the same time, we can question whether or not we have worked hard enough to surface and share these lessons with the next generation of leadership. If this book can be less of an oracle of new visions and more of a nautical chart for navigating toward an integrated leadership practice, then we will have earned the right to write about leadership.

We have been blessed with other wonderful trail guides who have shown us more integrated ways of thinking. Peter Checkland and Jay Forrester at MIT were two of the first to map the "systems dynamics, systems thinking, and soft systems" territory. Their work has helped us and thousands of leaders to frame the dynamic relationships and feedback loops present in every leadership challenge we face. As young academics their thoughts, along with the work of Karl Deutsch helped us to build a school for gifted seventeen-year-olds. Peter Senge, Ed Schein, and Arie De Geus introduced us and the world to "organization learning" so that we could begin to see systems as a useful management lens and apply the disciplines of systems thinking, dialogue, and scenario planning to our everyday management problems. Others with whom we have worked, such as Dana Zohar and Fritjof Capra have long ago described the relationship between inner consciousness and outward complexity, and signaled the need for leaders to pay attention to the lessons of "the new physics" and to a new view of consciousness if we are to grasp the leadership challenges of the next half century. Lastly, through our work with Bo Ekman and Charles Handy at the Tallberg Forum we are encouraged and inspired to share our unconventional perspective on leadership development, lest we become boiled frogs in an overheating pan called Earth.

It is a strong premise of this book that the valuable landmarks laid down by our forbears are at risk of being forgotten as the current mountain of research and writing piles up. We prefer frameworks that integrate the most compelling insights we can find so that we can place powerful knowledge and wisdom in the hands of our most gifted leaders. A few of those leaders, in the companies we serve, have compelled us to "keep it simple!" During the thousands of workshops we have delivered, they have told us again and again that their companies are overfull of frameworks, templates, and tools. Our canaries in the coalmines of global companies also report that "it all becomes too much to handle, does not lead to action, does not weave together what we already know." The "too much to handle" zone, or the "too hard box" as we called it during our time in Shell International, can be dangerous places on the landscapes. It is where the vector of decision making collapses into one dimension, where competing ideas are forced out, and "in-group" dynamics take over. It is a place where leaders escape to the safe ground of "simple solutions," "rational choices," and list making. Chris Argyris of the Monitor Group points out that when in doubt, leaders revert to their success formulae that, when reinforced, can become defensive routines fortified by labels such as "intuition" and "experience."

Landscapes can only provide a map of the terrain. We have tested out new maps of the landscapes with leaders to provide a way for them to reorient their priorities and place them in a wider context. But living and making use of a new landscape is not enough. We follow in the tradition of business intellectuals who are known for their mapping of the terrain: Edward De Bono and Charles Hampden-Turner who have encouraged the creative mapping of human behavior and creativity; Jon Katzenback, Chris Parker, and Eric van der Loo who have mapped the terrain of teams; Elliot Jacques who has explored the territory of organization that opened up the vistas for Morgan, Senge, Dawson, and others to follow; Henry Mintzberg, the late Sumantra Ghoshal, CK Prahalad, Chan Kim, and many more who pioneered the territory of the industry landscape and related it to other fields including the management of innovation; and colleagues at Shell and GBN who chose a different path based on their ability to take global scenarios and weave them into the implications for the other landscapes. These are but a few of the names along the trail to serve as guideposts for a more comprehensive view of the landscape. Why? Because on a practical, day-to-day level, we have found that most of the leaders who we have helped to prepare their backpacks for the journey had seen these different perspectives in a course, or an MBA program, or in a conference. But most of them had not integrated the insights into their practice, and few were willing to add another heavy book to their already loaded bags of experience. And like most of us the experiences they most learned from were their own mistakes and failures. Humbled by this understanding, we will try to provide a map for all leaders to place their particular experience, knowledge, and understanding in a wider context, with the challenge of keeping it simple enough for day-to-day practice.

How to read this book?

The structure of this book is created to feel like a journey to you, a journey on which you learn and a journey on which we are together with you as traveling companions. We might be guides at some points, but it is a journey on which we encourage your exploration. Regularly look out of the window, into the open field, and contemplate and reflect on what you are reading. Take your own time to undergo your journey, and make sure you relax sufficiently in between stops. There might be sites that you enjoy a lot, and would like to know more of. And there might be stops where you would say, "driver, please keep going." That's the good thing about our journey together, we are your guides, but you are in control of the destination. The real destination in this book is you, and what you can use and adopt, what you like and enjoy, what you experience and embody, and what you want to learn and practice.

So, we encourage you to engage in your journey in any way that works for you. We try to present insights, reflections, practices, and illustrations that will engage you. Reading the book from start to finish, and in that order, makes sense. Just as configuring your own journey out of the stops we provide makes sense. Here is just a brief description of the stops you can expect.

The core sites on our journey are the *leadership landscapes perspective* and the *equanimity shift* – others might call these "models" but we prefer to speak of them as perspectives. These perspectives capture the pivotal elements that we have found to be powerful in understanding and working on leadership skills. They are presented in Chapters 2 and 3. The *leadership landscapes perspective* represents the more analytical side of leadership, which we also label the "*seeing*" dimension of great leaders. The *equanimity shift* is the behavioral perspective we bring, one that uncovers five critical dimensions we have identified as the dimensions of great leadership. These are some edges for you to assess and work on. They encompass the "*being*" and "*doing*" sides of the leadership triangle we work from.

Having circled them in Chapter 3, we get off the bus and visit them in detail in Chapters 4 (*seeing*), 5 (*being*), and 6 (*doing*). We tour each of these revealing in more detail the *leadership landscapes perspective* and the *equanimity shift* of our previous chapters. While reading for an overview will suit many, there is enough to encounter here that some might want to take some time to reflect on the state of their own performance. We intend it to be a place to which you could return as you progress in your life's journey.

After Chapter 6, we continue our journey, and enter the practice field. If you have become inspired of what you visited, here is your chance to improve your edges. We start in Chapter 7 by realizing that there are *"moments of truth."* Metaphorically spoken of course, because these need not be instances, but could be longer periods of time. But we stick to the metaphor. It is in these moments of truth that your leadership is called for and that you can demonstrate your leadership. It is also in these moments that you can lose it or miss the opportunity to show your compatriots that there is a leader steering the ship. It is therefore pivotal that you learn to identify these moments and engage with them in the most powerful way.

Chapter 8 is about practice towards mastery. Just as you are about to enter the practice field, we invite you to envision the best teacher you have ever met. Someone who showed you a path towards mastery of a skill, a technique, a way of life. Think for a moment. Who is it? Is it a high school teacher, a former boss, a professor, a public figure, or one of your parents perhaps? With that person in mind, now imagine that she or he is standing there, at the side of the practice field. And as you are about to enter, you are called over, she or he coaches you:

> I'm very proud of what you have achieved. You've come a long way. Further than you ever imagined. And you will go much further, further than you can imagine right now. But do remember what gets you there. It's practice. Practice what you learn, practice what you feel, practice what you preach.

We close our journey with a gift from the tour guides: a wonderful story of the adventurous journey of Roald Amundsen at the start of the 20th century, as he navigated the Northwest Passage after 500 years of unsuccessful attempts by Europeans. We use this classical illustration to once more reiterate the important points we hope to give you throughout this book, as Roald Amundsen's great adventure is a tremendous illustration of phenomenal leadership, and is truly our "text book" example of all we would like to share with you on the subject of great leadership.

This is the journey that is ahead of you. You are invited to embark.

ACKNOWLEDGEMENTS

First and foremost we would like to acknowledge our families on both sides of the Atlantic for their care and support over the years that we spent taking long walks and weekends to gather our insights.

We would also like to thank our colleagues at Executive Learning Partnership, especially Nick van Heck and Ann de Jaeger for their business support and thoughts that went into this work. Additionally, we would like to give a nod to Mike Small who helped shape our early ideas and Tom Morley for his artistic talents. A special thanks goes to Rob-Jan de Jong for his dedication to the idea of Leadership Landscapes and for the drafting and editing that led to the completion of the project in written and web form.

Finally, we would like to thank the many, many people who have contributed to this project over the years – those with whom we have tested our ideas, shared in workshops, worked with in board retreats and dialogue. We invite you to visit our website at www.leadershiplandscapes.com where you will find a longer list of acknowledgements. If you find that a name that should have been acknowledged is missing from the list, please contact us at info@leadershiplandscapes.com.

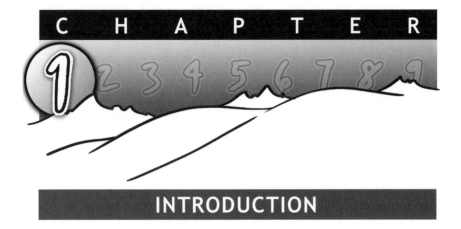

Introduction

In a breathtakingly high-paced world where some brave leaders are trying to drink from the fire hose of the Google,* a new set of leadership tools for their career might not be very helpful and may even draw the wrath of those who are already disoriented. It is for that reason that we have written a book that develops fresh concepts by building on and integrating a number of existing theories and tools. To do this we draw our inspiration from leadership in real time, from the real lives of existing leaders and those that are on the way to become the next generation of leaders. We have put ourselves in their shoes and wondered whether they need new tools and practices or whether they need a way to frame their lives. Or both.

Take, for example, Alex, a 42 year old Belgian Canadian business leader – one of the most confident people we know – who has served in postings from Sao Paulo to Seattle to Singapore, each one more successful than the last. His professional moves in the financial markets demonstrate substantial talent. Nominated to the management committee, a posting he has desired for nearly 20 years, he now considers his options.

His partner, Saskia, is also a leader in her field. She amazes people with her careful interpretations of corporate law. She is frequently demanded for testimony in New York and London, the headquarters of her recently

---

* As of this writing a search on "leadership" produced 163,000,000 citations in 0.1 seconds.

acquired firm. She has developed a mastery around conference calls for some of the biggest M&A deals in the world. Each deal reveals an artfully choreographed dance in a virtual world with global partners and clients. She knows the players. She controls the flow of the dance. She does not like to lose.

Saskia and Alex have two beautiful children in the proper schools, an au pair, and a half-a-million Euro mortgaged house in the right part of the village. Their double income makes it possible for them to go on expensive holidays. Everything perfect? No worries?

Even as we read these words we wait for the other shoe to drop. We anticipate another side to this story. Perhaps there are many possible "other sides" to this story. Yet consider that these other sides of the story may not be other sides at all but different aspects of the same landscape, different fractals of the same lives. Of course they want more. The trajectory of their lives points to more. At the same time doubts creep in, sometimes subtle, sometimes born of crisis. They know their capabilities, yet, increasingly a sense of limits dawns in their awareness or breaks into their consciousness:[1] limits to their own energy, limits to their ambitions, regrets at time away from home and family, and maintaining their finely tuned balances in the face of unrelenting demands and challenges.

Then there are the landscapes of performance. What's happening with the immediate work projects? What's going on with the teams they lead and the teams they are part of and with their relationships with colleagues and clients? How is all this affected by larger organizational concerns? How are they managing the limits of time and attention on these fronts?

And perhaps way in back of their minds lies more uncertainty regarding the limits and risks of the business cycles they are operating in and even limits to their belief that they can continue to do well and ignore the impact of their work on the social and ecological conditions in other parts of the world.

Saskia and Alex are not the only ones troubled with doubts like these. In our practice they come up regularly among current and aspiring leaders. A key developmental challenge of midcareer is how to step up to them, and a central challenge of sustainable leadership is how to remain engaged with them over the long haul.

In the face of these challenges some leaders take the approach of trying to do more and do it harder. Most who try more and harder find themselves sinking at the deep end of the pool swamped by energies that are overwhelmed, attention that has become unfocused or overfocused or dragged down by a tool kit that has become threadbare and heavy with predictability. Other leaders opt for simplicity by crowning one value king or by sacrificing one area of life to another.

1.1 A "considered" approach

The kind of leader we focus on takes a more considered approach that seeks integration and balance in the face of limits. This approach welcomes doubts as questions to be lived with and taken seriously. Our study of this "considered approach" to leadership has been oriented by questions such as, why do some leaders have an ability to integrate the landscapes of their work and lives while others do not? How do some leaders possess the composure to stay in balance yet adapt to changing circumstances? How does one build and sustain an integrated leadership practice that can both respond and adapt to the most urgent challenges while weaving their actions into a coherent framework – especially one that serves the world as the enduring signature of both their work life and their life's work?

Take the case of Christine Loh, a civic activist and business leader in Hong Kong. We visited Christine in Hong Kong in April 2007. Looking out across Hong Kong Harbor in the direction of Kowloon, the Star Ferry cuts a low bow wave that ripples out toward the bridge and off into the South China Sea. The boat is full, the streets are full, and life is full speed ahead in Hong Kong. A seemingly unstoppable force of human nature caught in a cycle of creative destruction and renewal. Centuries of history lock relationships into ritual and rivalry. Christine Loh knows. She was once an eager young trader working for a global investment bank, who wanted to learn skills that could be used to make a difference. Then at a certain moment she realized that any wealth she created could not be passed on in a proper way because the law forbade female involvement in the "males-only" inheritance laws. Over time she became a member of the Hong Kong legislative council. She led the charge that changed that law. In the meantime she saw other laws that excluded people, laws that led to unintentional consequences and simply "did not make sense."

Along the way, she developed a conscious practice to integrate her experiences, from the most spiritual to the most practical. When we asked Christine Loh to describe her considered approach she responded with an elegance that speaks to the core of what this book is about. "It is simple" she said.

Many of my colleagues see me working on a very diverse agenda, and wonder: how do you link it all together? How can you take so many diverse themes and find a red thread? How do you find balance in your varied lifestyle of travel, family, public policy and business leadership? I'm 51. That's important stage wise in terms of my perspective, my views, my understanding of people. I always try to maintain the big picture. But along with the big picture, I always need to verify. For that I go to the microcosm, and look for scenarios and shifts in the system. I find this intellectually exciting, as everything shifts all the time. I need to know how people feel, beyond the expert view. I know how to shape my presentations to serve multiple perspectives. I am genuinely excited when I am working with people to develop new hunches and then verify them – sometimes with very surprising results. At a recent conference I worked with a lighting engineer on the question of how we can price clean air. We had the same perspective coming from completely different worlds.

Are these skills and competences that everyone can learn? The most basic skill is to suspend the judgement part of my mind, the part that says "no" when I engage in a conversation or lead a workshop. People want to distil without listening. They want to map what is being said to their own experience. Can we learn how to suspend judgement, start with a "yes" and always feel excited about what is presented to us in a way that we feel "let's try it, or try to imagine the outcomes."

I have been deeply immersed in high profile issues that required me to change the interest structure. To do this I have had to stay one step ahead of the others and thoroughly understand the issues at hand. Inheritance rights involve history, politics, issues and awareness of the changing dynamics as this became a public issue. I admit that to handle that issue I had to exercise tremendous detachment to both keep physically healthy while constantly assessing new openings, new risks, while maintaining a situational awareness that could both pinpoint specific issues while showing that in the wider picture, there were much bigger issues at play. It is not just a moving target. You and others are shaping it at the same time.

Leaders who, like Christine Loh, take a considered approach live busy and full lives but for the most part do not seem particularly daunted by it all. They are clearly aware both of limits and of costs. They have achieved great heights yet hold their work and themselves in perspective. For Saskia and Alex the development of a more considered approach could be the best way to catch the shoe as it is dropping.

1.2   Two main ideas

There are two main, interrelated ideas that lie at the heart of this considered approach. The first is an image of a landscape. It is a natural metaphor to draw our attention to an emerging view of leadership in a world where everything connects, at speed, to everything and everyone else. At the same time, by having an integrated view, expressed through landscapes, we can find fresh words and images to support a new generation of leaders who, in our care, are looking for inspiration, clarity, and direction. This group, many of whom are already masters in their fields of work and occupation, shows us their fatigue and dislike for management frameworks that have too many dimensions, too many variables, and too many choices when navigating in an increasingly connected world. It is through our development work with many fine leaders that we have come to know their practices and understand their emergent ways of working. For them we strive to share some of their signposts and milestones along the way and link the disparate roadmaps to an overall image of the leadership landscape.

A second and important aspect of the considered approach is to take enough time to explore the inner landscapes of leaders' work and lives so that the reader can place their stories into a new perspective. Through our research on the qualities that sustain leaders and hold them to their wider commitments, we discover that a part of the genius of leaders such as Juan Rada at Oracle, Rattan Chada at Mexx, or Christine Loh at Hong Kong's Civic Exchange is their unique ability to hold the foreground while staying conscious of wider perspective on the landscape and, when necessary, to reconfigure and rapidly rebalance in the face of new challenges and trade-offs. In every case, this "rapid recovery" did not come without powerful experiences and conscious practice. It was often developed through the integration of their learning into a wider frame of life's experiences that helped them to "make sense" of what happened while "feeling a shift" in their perspective. They became conscious of what they were doing – and then were able to develop a mastery of a different sort.

In this book we do not dwell on complexity and turn it into a nemesis of every choice or situation that leaders face. Instead we choose to recognize the "buzzing, blooming reality" present in every organization and boardroom we visit. Our purpose is not to shy away from complexity but to consider more hidden pathways through the maze. Throughout our narrative, we draw attention to masterful leaders whose art form is their ability to see and stay open to a rich mix of colors and broad strokes across the landscape, while sustaining a presence of mind for the details of their most pressing challenges.

1.3 Seeing, being, and doing

This has led us to the notion that leaders need to build maps of the landscape that help them to discover and "see" where they currently put their energy and attention. Through collaborative map-making one recovers a perspective on one's work and life. We explain that the next logical step in the leader's journey is to make conscious choices about where one wants to "be" in terms of intentions and commitments, before deciding what to "do." The sequence of "seeing," "being," and "doing" takes us to our central thesis: if leaders fail to combine an understanding of the wider landscape, their sense of where they are playing most power-fully, and the capacity to stay in balance, they have not entered the black belt level of leadership mastery.

We invite you to a new practice field for leaders, a gymnasium that starts with the art of rebalancing, of living comfortably in continuous motion on the landscapes of our work and our lives. We challenge you as a reader to develop your own unique and creative path back to equa-nimity or to use another phrase, to seek your own "dynamic balance" through some well-described practices. The masters of these integrative leadership practices have shown us the way. It is our ambition to capture the essence of their ideas, place it in a business context, and share it with a wider public. For some it will be a useful tool box, for others it has become a way of life.

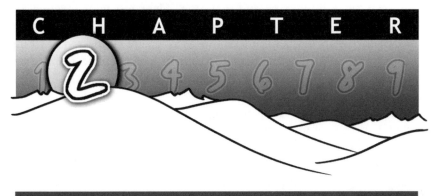

Leadership Landscapes

It was up in the Rose Center in the American Museum of Natural History when the quarter dropped for me. It was one of those moments in life when the "obvious" gets presented, yet I needed the universe to see it. We had been waiting for our turn at the Hayden Planetarium with my – then 10-year-old – son, and as we entered the space of "the largest and most powerful virtual reality simulator in the world" and gazed in full amazement, shock, and excitement at the star-filled ceiling of this enormous room, the "outer-body" experience led me to my realization. You will surely need the virtual reality (VR) simulator for that, but let me help you imagine.

Imagine a clear night's sky filled with stars. Assume you are away from all the busy-ness, in a place all by yourself, without false lights, noises, or any other distractions. Think of yourself gazing at that sky and seeing the distant stars. In a fully relaxed position, your eyes face up, completely filling your eyesight with the universe. Surely your mind wanders off into the immeasurable vastness of the picture before you. Go as far out as you can and see the stars that appear furthest away. Explore what they look like, how they shape, how they illuminate, how they radiate, what they tell you. Then move toward the ones that are closer, some that seem immediate, like large luminous snowflakes. If you are lucky, you might even see a few falling stars, and now that this is just your imagination anyway, just imagine this as well. Imagine that all of these points of light, snowflakes to stars and all the strata in-between are connected, forming a tremendous web, creating an interdependent map of connection points. And although each individually appears to stand alone, in this picture, none of them actually seems to stand alone.

Is that not just like the world of relationships, the highly interconnected world that leaders must navigate in every day?

If you really put yourself in that picture, *really* allow your imagination to lead you there, it might be awe-inspiring; you may really feel connected to all that, truly feel peaceful and relaxed within yourself, and feel energized by the picture that emerges in front of you. In fact, just imagining this picture might already be a source of inspiration that recharges your batteries. Or it might feel overwhelming, disorienting, overly impressive, and frankly, just too much. Particularly if you were trying to locate where you stand and to make your way within such a dazzling field of connections.

When I stood there at Hayden Planetarium, listening to the voice of Tom Hanks as he took us to the far ends of our universe, I realized that leadership had become relational. The myth of the leader as a standalone act is finished.

2.1   Leadership is relational

Leadership has always been relational. Great leaders have held a view of the horizon and what is over it and have been able to articulate the vision of purpose that stirs a sense of shared meaning so that people can understand how their current efforts relate to the goals at the horizon. So in that sense, there is nothing new. Or is there?

We charge leaders with the responsibility to navigate our organizations with their stakeholders through the demands of the outside world, across a competitive field, and more and more in the wider context of our societies. While at the same time, we expect our leaders to craft the organization, to manage their leadership team, and perhaps most essential, to manage themselves as healthy, vibrant, clear-thinking, and inspiring individuals.

Is that not what we expect from our leaders today? But how is this different from what it used to be? Well, several aspects are fundamentally different since our world in recent times has shifted to a place where we have not been before. We find ourselves living in a world that seems to be turning ever faster on its axis, bombarding us with information in ever larger doses and at ever increasing speeds. At this pace, the points of light in the sky assume a dizzying whirl. In particular, the technologies that have emerged over the last two decades have driven us to places unknown before, inflicting fundamental business shifts such as globalization, 24-hour economies, and empowered clients, suppliers, and other stakeholders, to mention just a few of these changes. And as we are starting to come to grips with the business rules and dimensions that come with these changes, the leadership we expect has clearly shifted significantly as well.

If previously leadership was compared to a chess game, in which with mastery and deft analysis we make our moves across the chess board, making decisions and choices that define our own path to success, leadership nowadays can be better compared to a game of squash or racket ball, where there is little time to think, where instincts rule, and with a ball that can come from any direction. It is a game that requires navigation, speed, and a significant dose of physical and mental health and agility to play along. And yet we know that in a more complex environment flying by the seat of the pants is not enough.

Are we asking too much of our leaders? Certainly possible. Squash and racket ball are not everyone's game. One way of coping with the complex surround of relationships is to ignore the complexity and go for the simple "just do it." There are too many variables, too many relationships, so just get on with it, set course, drive, and lead! This strategy can look good in the short run – at least it gives the impression of having a confident hand on the wheel. It certainly is a popular perspective for leaders who have been used to a hierarchical model, and surely there are still plenty of those out there.

But it only works until the intervening variables that were ignored and the unintended consequences that might have been foreseen, start to become obvious. And by that time things may be unfolding beyond our control. This behavior has long been inadequate – now it has become dangerous. Without new ways of looking at how we lead, we are bound to fall short of the needs and expectations of those who follow us.

Remember the case of Brent Spar? Shell's PR disaster of the century has been well published and needs few words to say what went wrong as the conflict between Shell and Greenpeace unfolded in 1995. Throughout the episode I was constantly reminded of my own experience with Shell two years before. As a young planner in Shell, I was asked to set up a competency framework for the Corporate HR function. It was in that capacity that I interviewed the person responsible for Shell's Public Affairs and asked him the question "What are you doing to include your public stakeholders?". Proudly he answered:

Well, we actually have an excellent process for that. We hold an active dialogue with our stakeholders: we go out and visit them twice a year. We interview them, and collect their views and perspectives on our business and our company. We bring those perspectives together, analyze where we stand at that point, what has changed, and report that back, in our semi-annual report, to senior management. So, we have a very good data-driven understanding of what our stakeholders need, and through this mechanism, we can assure that everyone in the organization is brought up-to-date with the perspectives of our stakeholders, and can decide where and how intervention is needed.

Fantastic – just as the textbook on stakeholder management would tell you to do. But how come Shell failed so miserably two years later? Well, this serves as an example that goes to the roots of how leadership has shifted. What is at the heart of this story is that Shell, despite all its adequate processes and intentions, failed to understand that in the new era that was entered in the mid-1990s, stakeholders had no interest in how Shell managed their internal processes. Stakeholders no longer accepted – nor needed to accept – the internal processes that served organizations so well, until relationships became fundamentally more important. As Shell had become part of a web of interconnecting lights, stakeholders wanted to know instantly how Shell was going to be responsive to their needs. It was no longer accepted that stakeholders had to live with the rules of the organization, as the organization-centric perspective was shifting to a relationship-centric model, in which feelings and action were as important as data collection, and where the on-going contact with stakeholders was as important as its outcomes.

It illustrates how leadership in the "old model," which placed the organization in the middle of attention and derived its strategies and actions from there, has now become part of an integrated management discipline that goes beyond the divisions of labor we had learned from our Taylorian legacies.

2.2   Leadership landscapes master perspective

Successful leaders negotiate the world that is emerging before our eyes by grasping the multifaceted surround and the relational nature of leadership. It is this new – or more immediate – feature of leadership that must be attended to, because the new reality cannot be ignored. So rather than assuming we are asking too much of leaders today, what they really need is a perspective to sort through the complexities of the relationships and identify the points in the web that matter most at a given time.

If relational leadership has come to the forefront, would it not be of great value to have a "tool base" that helps us navigate between the landscapes of the world outside the organization and the world inside? A perspective that acknowledges the horizon-scanning role of leadership, yet also acknowledges the drivers, needs, and intents of the organization, the team, and certainly also, a leader's individual needs.

At the same time, we recognize that it must not lead to oversimplification or come at the price of losing the sense of the whole field in which the unforeseen, interweaving variables continue to emerge and play a role. It should confirm that leadership is relational and provide a way to deal more effectively with the relationships, whatever their nature is, while increasing our ability to get things done fast.

We will make the case in the intervening pages that the *leadership landscape perspective* is one of the two core pillars that stand underneath successful leadership in the age we live in. It is the pillar of *"seeing"* that is pivotal to great leadership. Because only those who can see reality from a larger perspective, reframe issues to provide clarity and coherence, and maintain an eye for possibility and everything that goes with it, can grow to master level. Leading without providing perspective is not leading at all. It is the leader's role, task, and responsibility to provide a future-oriented direction, regardless of whether we label it with a big word such as "vision," or a more modest term such as "perspective." Without the ability to "see" into the future, and make sense of it for oneself and others, it will be impossible to sustain a leadership position effectively.

But first a surgeon's warning: as with any sound framework, it looks straightforward and simple at first, possibly even too straightforward for some. But it is our mission in this book to uncover the hidden depths of it, to show you how it can provide direct and indirect support to your leadership skills, and expose the edges to your work, so you can aspire to reach "master level."

Let us explore what it looks like.

Suppose that you already have an organizing principle for how you lead. If your job is marketing, you focus on marketing. If it is planning, then you plan. Finance, well, it is clear. But have you considered that beyond your discipline, your role, your tasks, and even your job, that your work lives in a rich set of "seated relationships" that form the relational web of your work and life.

Imagine you are perched on a vista ("your job") looking out across the peaks and valleys. What you might see is *the macro-business landscape* – the landscape that primarily deals with the wider context of the business environment – it is beyond the competitive field, and deals with the organization's role in society and the world at large. Typical focal points here are sustainability, emerging technologies, political systems, NGOs, the broader regulatory environment, social responsibility, environmental concerns, social (im)balances, and so on. Increasingly they include the global economy and the planetary environment. These are the mountains in the background that

LEADERSHIP LANDSCAPES MASTER PERSPECTIVE

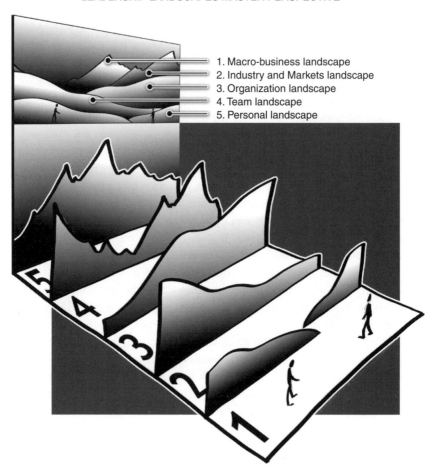

1. Macro-business landscape
2. Industry and Markets landscape
3. Organization landscape
4. Team landscape
5. Personal landscape

will have a tremendous business impact, yet are often less immediate and sometimes less direct then the sharper peaks and valleys of *the industry and markets landscape*. Here we find challenges that relate to our direct external business context, such as demanding customers, changing markets, shifting competition, and our most direct stakeholders (e.g. investor relations).

Yet according to our research, few leaders dwell long on the lofty heights, because they are pulled into the morass of *the organization landscape*. This landscape mainly deals with issues of organizational concern, such as how we will govern, how we attract and distribute resources, how we org-chart our people, how we set-up, maintain, and live our culture and values, and how we keep the organization aligned and informed. And subsequently, there are bands of brothers and sisters on *the team landscape*, who require our attention. This is where we manage the team, steer it, chair meetings, do appraisals, ensure recruitment and personal development, and improve team performance. Finally, we come to the nearest environment, *the individual landscape*, where we cover our time spent on ourselves – our development and learning, reflection, coaching, meditation, and other activities where we maintain and strengthen our own physical and mental health.

Right through the book, we will refer to the *leadership landscapes perspective*, and place you as a leader in it, to relate the key lessons we have learned from our own journeys through the landscapes. We invite you to join us for this integrative perspective and approach.

2.3 The most valuable leadership currency: leadership attention units

The five landscapes cover the areas where "leadership attention" is typically spent by any leader in any business organization. We will refer to the term "leadership attention units" (LAU) throughout this book, as it nicely describes a kind of currency. What it has in common with a dollar, euro, yen, and any other currency is that it can only be spent once. Your LAUs are therefore of natural scarcity, which makes it more and more important that you spend your LAUs wisely across the landscapes.

LAUs are – by the way – a great way of measuring where one's time is spent, as well as where one's defaults lay. At http://www.leadership-landscapes.com we provide a straightforward diagnostic that measures your spending of LAUs and how that relates to your defaults. It is very interesting to find your profile, gaps, and benchmarks, as it can be very insightful to see how your collective team spends their time, whether that leaves gaps, and how that benchmarks against others in your sector. You will find more on how this works, and can work for you, in our Chapter 8, where we uncover five ways to integrate the ideas set forth in this book through a set of straightforward practices.

2.4 Functions of the leadership landscapes perspective

The *leadership landscapes perspective* serves to provide structure to the inter- and intralandscape relationships. It serves as

an atlas to locate the landscapes of action within the wider field of view.

a navigator that reminds an executive to shift focus from one landscape to another.

a presencing device to show up powerfully at critical moments as leaders work across different landscapes.

a lens for zooming in, out, around, and across the landscapes, and to telescope from an individual landscape back to grasping the entirety.

a balancing function, to monitor and track if and how different landscapes are dealt with over time and at any moment by oneself as well as one's team.

2.4.1   ATLAS FUNCTION

A typical atlas of the world begins with a map of the whole globe, followed by maps of territories and countries. Imagine a virtual atlas in which the view of the whole is the surround we met at the outset of this chapter. Then imagine within this three-dimensional surround the outlined shapes of more bounded terrains. Among the wide number of such territories we might identify a few that stand out as classic contexts  of leadership – the organization, the team or boardroom, the marketplace, and the industry. Others are equally obvious but often ignored in theories on leadership – the leader's own life, the societal matrix, and the global, multifaceted surround.

2.4.2 NAVIGATOR FUNCTION

Where the atlas function helps identify where we are, the navigator function helps to find and maintain the path through the territory. As the old army saying goes: "the map is not the territory." Moving forward requires the atlas function, but also requires a pathseeker that helps identify the most suitable path, drawing on a complete picture. When we do not have the full picture in mind, the path will become selected from one dimension only, such as the fastest path, or the lowest cost path. With all the landscapes involved in the decision-making process, alternative paths come to mind that would not have been seen originally, as for example the most innovative path or the path that engages most of the organization in the process. These are paths that come up as the issue at hand is viewed from the holistic, all landscapes perspective. The navigator function therefore moves the atlas forward into the guide to action.

2.4.3 PRESENCING DEVICE

The presencing function of the landscape master perspective supports leaders in a stance of dynamic balance wherever they show up. We will go into the specifics of dynamic balance in the next chapter, but for now it is useful to understand that presencing is a key leadership quality we identify. In its most direct form, presencing is about how we show up and how we focus our attention.

Used across the landscapes, presencing finds different meaning on different landscapes, yet it is all related to how one uses presence to lead. At the *team landscape* for instance, practicing presence is in the service of building trust and mutuality with each team member. Exercising presence starts by being alert to the dynamics of the team, driving toward optimal performance and synergies, while leading the team in creating, living, and telling the story of its members' mutual journey.

2.4.4   ZOOMING LENS FUNCTION

A paradox expressed by leaders we work with is that others demand that they place their attention on a specific part of the landscape, while they are conscious that the specific challenge is often linked to one or more other fields of view. The masterful leader understands how to stay focused on the challenge at hand, while telescoping back to a wider frame of reference. In doing so,

the whole context comes into view, as a telephoto lens that moves from the specific bird in a tree to the whole tree full of birds, and then back to the individual subject. Powerful speakers use telescoping techniques. A speaker can make a powerful generalization by drawing attention to an individual or a team that epitomizes the point. On the contrary, by drawing a team's work into the wider mission and the challenges of an industry, the work at hand is enabled and becomes more relevant for the members of the team. The very practiced leaders we have known have a remarkable capacity to hold the entire landscape in perspective and telescope their holistic view to a specific, well-timed action.

2.4.5   BALANCING FUNCTION

Every leader has default landscapes; one, two, or even three that they get drawn to most of the time. By noticing where you actually spend your time, and setting this off against your natural defaults, a profile will emerge that leads to further insight in your balances and how you spend your LAUs. Surely, the balance need not to be perfect, and is at any moment situational, so that the

balance between natural defaults and actual time spent on other landscapes is not perfectly aligned. Yet, sustained imbalance can lead to untapped leadership resources, or worse, to ineffectiveness and loss of morale.

As we know, the people you lead have a built-in antenna that detects whether or not their leader is paying attention to one landscape or another and have an advanced sensitivity device as to whether their leader is responsive to the needs and requirements they have at their landscapes.

2.5   Case study

We are rarely masterful at shifting our effort and attention across the landscapes. This requires energy, will, and practice. Some of these are primary functions of our master perspective itself; others are explorations to further develop the core feature of our master perspective: holistic leadership. We will go into these practices in much more detail in Chapter 8, but as a starter, we will uncover first, a deceptively simple yet very powerful way of gaining a much wider perspective, a practice called *inquiry mapping*.

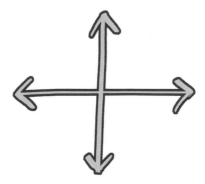

For a full account on how to do *inquiry mapping*, we refer to the second practice in Chapter 8. At this point, we just say that an inquiry map is a four-dimensional map used to explore a topic on a given landscape in further detail. The four dimensions to explore are situational, and you are by no means forced to use any prescribed set. Therefore, *inquiry mapping* is a generic approach (yet to help you explore we provide some useful suggestions for powerful dimensions in section 8.2). The aim of this practice is to provide a quick way of getting a much richer picture around a subject (a challenge, dilemma, and so on), so that a better informed and better considered decision can be made. This way we can engage with the complexity of a given landscape without losing the sense of the complexity. It becomes manageable as an analog for the complexity.

Our generic approach is based on our experience that, when you work with more than four dimensions, complexity gets overwhelming and it is hard to progress in your understanding. If you use less than four, you risk oversimplifying or overgeneralizing the issue at hand, which hurts your sense making as well. Therefore, for generic *inquiry mapping* we use four dimensions. If you frame your issue in terms of the four most powerful dimensions, and consider all of the other dimensions of the problem as background, then you can bring them forward as needed.

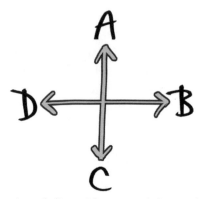

Reducing to four pivotal dimensions – and determining which they are according to your sense of importance and impact – is your first win. Your second win is when you start exploring how each of your key dimensions relates to each other. So, you consider the (six) relationships that your dimensions have (A with B, A with C, A with D, B with C, B with D, and C with D). This second step of looking at the issue from an integrated perspective almost always provides key insights that were not considered before. Where we are typically aimed at isolating a dimension from all the others – to free ourselves from the complexity – we hereby propose to look at the issue directly from the four key dimensions, and the six inter-relationships between the dimensions. This provides an integrated per-spective rather than an isolated perspective, and it will help you approach key issues in a different, much richer, yet coherent way.

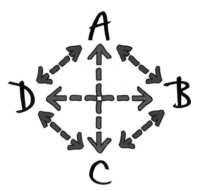

Among the board members and leaders we have worked with over the years, most will admit, in a quiet conversation, that the challenge of their work is not the work itself, but the choices they must make on a minute-by-minute, week-by-week, month-by-month basis about where to place their energies and attention. Many will play their strong hand and play where they are most gifted. Others behave in a way that could be more called "the dolphin" approach: the leader dives in to grab an issue and springs back out of the water before others have resolved it, presenting them with a *fait accompli*. What such approaches have in common is that they do not provide, or include, working on the issue from a larger perspective. It is the "just-do-it" approach that rules, which is neither stimulating and inspiring to the team, nor taps into the knowledge and insights of the team by engaging with the issue from a complete perspective.

By working with executives to help them grasp the whole landscape, using the *leadership landscapes perspective* in combination with *inquiry mapping*, we first make them become more conscious about where they place their energies. Subsequently, by providing an easily applicable, generic approach to broaden and deepen the perspective at the same time, they expressed a sense of gratification and completion that they had rarely experienced in their busy lives.

Let us see now how it works in real life. A case study will help us to grasp what comes next.

2.5.1 CASE: OUTSOURCING

At the beginning of last year, Sam Ellison (fictional name) was assigned a "bet the company" job to make "smart sourcing" or "outsourcing" work for a large part of the back office functions in his financial institution. The project spanned the globe, requiring tough negotiations with his service provider in Bangalore, difficult conversations with unions at home, and a transformation project that would start at the head office and eventually touch the lives of thousands of people. Two outsourcing projects had been started before, and both had stalled; one was because the technology was not mature enough for the complex tasks of insurance and banking and therefore deemed too high risk, and the second was that the unions in Germany signaled that they would refuse thousands of layoffs or displacing people from one company to another and away from Germany to another EU country.

Sam was confronted with a bewildering array of choices and possibilities that stretched him to the limits of his 24 years of experience as a senior Information Management executive. By the time we caught up with Sam, he was nearly ready to hand the job back to the board and ask for a reassignment, even though it would be a black mark on his otherwise unscathed career path.

He called the team together, and we introduced them to the idea that they were working on a transformation project that would have an impact across the landscapes of the work and lives of many, including themselves. We next introduced them to our toolset of *leadership landscapes* and *inquiry mapping* to grasp the challenges they were facing on each landscape, and to help them move themselves and their teams away from growing disorientation and confusion to clear insights about the next steps to take on their journey.

After a few minutes of team discussion, it was clear that most of the challenges they described were on the landscape of the organization, so we naturally went to that landscape first. Note that we start at the place where the team is putting most of its energy and attention, not because it is the most important landscape, but because it is the door they chose to enter. Of course there were challenges on other landscapes, particularly in the area of team dynamics. But those could be tackled in subsequent conversations. First things first.

We began by asking: "What are the most critical challenges that this project faces on the landscape of the organization?" The following list appeared (reduced for this example):

▶ buy-in from the users;
▶ overcoming fears that outsourcing would change the culture;
▶ concerns about who would get what jobs;
▶ lots of issues around process mapping to know which jobs were internal and which would be outsourced;
▶ questions about the level of skills in the company to deal with the new systems requirements.

Once the list was completed we took a break. One of the team members rushed to us to say: "This is great. Lets just complete the list, prioritize it, and start tackling the issues, one by one."

For many leaders, this would be the logical next step. We ignored his advice. Why? Many teams, at this point fall into what one wag characterized as the "New Year's Resolution Trap." Each year, on December 31, many people make a list of resolutions that they will tackle in the following year. One of them is usually related to being more fit or healthy in the coming year. No problem here. Yet by about late February early March, the jogging routine has stopped, or the new diet plan has stalled, or the fancy equipment causes unforeseen pain, or the new relationship takes more time, and so on and so forth. The main problem of making a list is not lack of will or self-discipline. Believe it or not, the biggest problem is that everything was placed in a list and each issue is tackled as a separate item on a list, and not seen as an array of challenges that have a relationship to one another. In other words:

Many of the challenges we face in our businesses and our lives are not the challenge itself, but the issues that arise from competing challenges and interests.

When the session reconvened we drew a simple inquiry map with some archetypical organization dimensions:

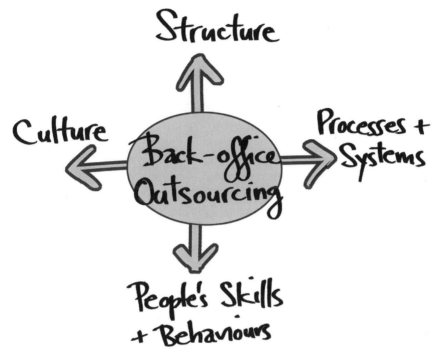

We then listed all of the issues that they had raised under each of these headings and began a conversation that started with all of the structural challenges. We proceeded with a series of questions that focused on each part of the *inquiry map*:

▶ Where are you spending most of your time, energy, and attention? (Answer: structure, processes, and systems)
▶ What does this project have to do with changing the culture? (at first, no response, then lively discussion)
▶ Will there be new skills required? (Answer: yes, and people some-how have to magically acquire them, and this issue can wait – whereas it was later admitted that it was a higher priority than thought).

Next we explored the "interimpacts" of the issues. This is when the real powerful stuff appeared:

▶ How is your time spent on structure, processes, and systems having an impact on the culture?

▶ What will be the long-term impact of outsourcing processes and systems on the skills and behaviors required in the future back office of the organization? Who is building this map?

▶ How are outsourced processes and systems going to affect the culture of the organization now and in the long run?

As these questions started to surface, the discussion became very lively and rich, as they were making connections between the four dimensions all the time. Sometimes a combination of dimensions resulted in a new perspective, sometimes a discussion about how to appropriately balance the dimensions emerged, sometimes timing (or prioritization) comments were recorded, and so on. An outsider would have observed that the group had very rapidly moved from a "list-handling" approach, to an integrated approach, taking a rich set of dimensions into account in their discussion, without getting overwhelmed by the complexity.

From the *inquiry mapping* discussion on the landscape of organization three things emerged that were of direct practical relevance for all:

1. The dialogue around the sets of issues on the landscape surfaced hidden biases and assumptions in the team about what was important.
2. They began to see that if they did not tackle the "interimpacts" of their arrayed issues, they would be working on the wrong stuff.
3. More important than making lists was to consider the right sequencing of moves that would help them tackle the issues in relation to one another, rather than as singularities.

Once we had gone to the heart of the issues on the landscape of the organization, we got back into the helicopter and went to the wider perspectives of the other landscapes – the individual, team, industry, and global. We asked:

"What has our conversation surfaced that challenges our assumptions about how we look at the whole spectrum of the landscape?"

Their responses showed that they were beginning to see their challenges in what Peter Senge likes to call a "Whole Systems Perspective."[1] They reported: "This certainly challenges how we have made team assignments," "I'm not sure our original assumptions about what our competitors are doing with their back offices is still valid," "Do we have a strong enough understanding of how things will develop in India to ensure we are not exposed in terms of our data integrity, resourcing or increasing costs driven by demand from other players?" and many more of such "whole perspective" questions.

From the helicopter view it was straightforward to dive back down to the individual landscapes, employing *inquiry mapping* at each level.

Originally, we experienced the same sort of reluctance as we had at the start of the conversation (when we had our list that "merely" needed prioritization). The sentiment was that the issue was now well viewed, based on the rich discussion they had on the organization landscape, and it was hard to imagine there was more to be said. Regardless, we did flip to the next landscape.

As we went through each of the landscapes, in several cases, such as industry dynamics, when we looked at first glance, it appeared not to be relevant to the most pressing challenges facing the team. Yet, over time, they began to see that their challenges were embedded in a context of issues that were arrayed across the landscapes and that without the context, they could get disoriented or misunderstand the issue in its narrow perspective.

Within a half day we had flown across the wider perspectives of the landscapes, and telescoped down to the terrain to map out the territory and reconsider the issues in the light of the wider perspective. At the end of the session their feedback was clear: "Simple without oversimplifying!," "I now have a context for my decision making," and "we were at risk of making the wrong decisions because we did not see them in relation to other issues."

Inquiry mapping within and across the landscapes of our leadership agenda is a powerful step toward integrated leadership and provides a way to face the complexity of our business challenges with new eyes and powerful insights.

2.6 Integrated leadership

We see integrated – or holistic – leadership as a leader's ability to navigate across the landscapes with grace and confidence. As our case study demonstrates, there is tremendous richness in gaining the widest perspective on a specific issue and in looking at issues in a relational map. Many insights do not get uncovered, or thought and spoken about, by taking a challenge merely on its own landscape. Taking the relationships with the other landscapes into account, a much richer picture emerges of the issue at hand, which adds to the integrative perspective.

Integrative thinking is the worldview we bring to the expedition. It is our understanding of the world. It's how we make sense of what goes on. If a simple mechanistic worldview is the equivalent of the flat earth society, an integrative approach is one which, by contrast, recognizes the varied topography, broad range of ecosystems, and multitude of terrains we shall encounter. The earth is round and our vision of it is rounded, it declares.

As integrative thinkers we struggle to see the whole problem, embrace, and inhabit its multivaried nature, and try to comprehend the complexity of its causal relationships. We would search for creative resolutions to problems seen by others as irreducible.

It seems obvious that this is the best way to think and act, so what stops us doing so? Why does not everyone "think integratively?" Maybe it is because we live in a world that stands in the way of efforts to integrate. It has become a fact of life that our world is highly complex and riddled with ambiguity. Yet our outlook on life is often characterized by a linear, one dimensional, and highly fragmented view of "how things stand." This serves to provide us with a sense of clarity, which falsely feels like the best we can do given the inherent complexity. It is therefore easy to suffer from a sort of systematic blindness. Compounding this we often react from a position of an ingrained defensiveness – a basic insecurity that drives us toward thinking: "I'm right and you're wrong." A sort of dualism is hardwired into our worldview and hampers an integrative approach.

An integrated way of thinking inevitably means to see beyond the foreground and in terms of intergenerational legacies and stewardships to simultaneously see all the key dimensions of an issue or challenge. But this goes against a wider cultural malaise that much of western society suffers from. That is, our outlook has been dominated by short termism in production planning and politics, in business and organizational structures. The cumulative effect of this short-term approach is witnessed for example in the ecological crises we face, as we do not know how to place the wider issues in the perspective of our day-to-day leadership.

Efforts towards more integrative thinking are a response to the wider criticism of the destructive impact of "instrumental reason," the dominant worldview which uses reason only as a tool to reach the goals, not to say which goals are right. The point is that the failure to think integratively is not a minor lapse of little consequence, but a failure we see played out around us in a world of disjuncture, missed opportunity, and unfulfilled potential at a societal level, at a business level, and at a level that affects our leadership legacy.

The integrative approach we advocate is therefore largely motivated by a need to move from fragmented behavior – a constant reaction to crisis and responding to the issues as separate – toward intentional holistic behavior in leadership – learning by design, theory, and practice.

Perhaps we should examine more closely where integrated thinking derives from, before looking at some leadership examples of where this approach can lead us.

2.6.1   ROOTS OF INTEGRATION

Some virtuous intellectual attitudes including *tolerance, empathy, openness,* and *freedom of speech* can be seen as forerunners of an integrative attitude. We can see the roots of this way of thinking in the evolution of biology from a molecular to a systems theory, in moves to whole-systems thinking in education or in the growing understanding of holistic health practice.[2]

Perhaps at the heart of this groundswell toward integrative thinking has been the emerging field of ecology that needed by definition to develop and define units of study that went beyond individual organisms, leading to ideas of plant assemblages, communities, and even superorganism groups.

Integrative thinking is an intellectual method, applied in thinking and communication, enabling a constructive synthesis between apparently incompatible, conflicting, or unrelated visions. This related to some of the discussion we will have in the remainder of the book on diversity and the vitality brought about by multiple viewpoints. It evokes the memory of the American philosopher and psychologist William James who wrote:

> Hands off: neither the whole of truth nor the whole of good is revealed to any single observer, although each observer gains a partial superiority of insight from the peculiar position in which he stands.[3]

In a leadership context this allows us to *approach* problems rather than *solve* them in a dichotomous fashion. It allows us to see possibility. As the leadership development master Ian McMonagle maintains: *"We need to stalk our problems like a lion stalks its prey before we pounce."*

This integrated technique stands in contrast to the dominance of a critical approach, which often consists of breaking the problem down into parts, looking for past data about each of the individual parts, analyzing that data for trends, and then checking and sometimes copying what others have done before. This approach is methodical but also limiting, routine, and unimaginative. It is not appropriate for individuals facing multiple choices and ranges of choices when these choices cannot be made from within narrowly prescribed or operational divisions.

At a more profound level, integrative thinking is a response to the widespread rejection of dualism. The traditional, scientific paradigm argues that, in the presence of two or more incompatible hypotheses, only one can be "true." Hypotheses conflicting with the "true" one, are obligatorily "false." This theory obeys ancestral Aristotelian and Cartesian rules that state that assertions are either true or false, and that an assertion, conflicting with a true one, is necessarily false. In this worldview that we have inherited, "thinking" primarily consists of "falsification" that is checking which hypothesis is true and which is false, and intellectual labor consists of proving or refuting hypotheses.

On the contrary, the integrative approach presupposes that, most probably, conflicting assertions can be largely true, and that the apparent incompatibility of conflicting concepts is rather due to overgeneralized or overconcretized details, or to the position of the observer, while the essence of each knowledgeable contribution most probably *is* true. Does this mean everything is just reduced to a sort of passive equivalence? Not at all. Of course hard decisions will still have to be made, but these can be made in the context of rich information and diverse opinions arrayed before us across the leadership landscapes.

A key form of relevant intellectual work consists more in trying to resolve these apparent incompatibilities by reformulating our source hypotheses and assumptions so as to keep the common elemental truth and drop unjustified exaggerations. This work aims toward a construction that integrates the compatible parts of the formerly conflicting assertions into a workable outcome. We think of this most commonly found form as "pragmatic integration."

Another classic form of integration is the formation of a fundamentally new superseding synthesis out of a variety of elements including those of both conflicting concepts. This dialectal approach to integration with roots in classical Greece and generally associated with the philosophy of Hegel continues as a key concept in thinking about how the world is reshaped over time.[4]

A third approach involves constructing a unifying framework spacious enough to encompass irreducibly conflicting truths so that incompatibilities can be recognized and bridged at least until further means of integration are discovered. A classic example of this is the circle containing within it the symbols of yin and yang, which communicates polarities interdepending within a larger unity.

One other interesting contrast between the dominant worldview of instrumental reason and the fresh approach we advocate is that integrative thinking is intrinsically about dialogue. It is a social way of thinking because our mission is not to refute your answers or your approach but to understand what is good and useful in them.

This is not to reduce all contentious issues and varying approaches to a sort of theoretical mush; clearly there are times and instances when theories or ideas are plain wrong, ethically questionable, or morally indefensible. The point is more that the *raison d'être* of one's entire worldview is no longer based on refuting an "opposing" argument or theory.

Integration is a process of synthesizing or relating in an integrated frame. Our approach allows valuable contributions and creative but embryonic ideas to be salvaged rather than discarded.

This is why we encourage leaders to take an integrated perspective. We all know that is not a one-person task; the most successful leaders are those who focus on letting the team excel. They foster multiple perspectives and manage to create an integrative outcome to the challenges faced. Yet, why do we still come across leaders who try to control their teams, block out competing perspectives, and divide and conquer wherever possible? Our observations on the art of leadership are echoed in the qualities of Level 5 Leadership described by Jim Collins, in his landmark study *Good to Great: Why Some Companies Make the Leap ... and Others Don't*.

Collins found that the leaders of those few organizations that stood out significantly in terms of performance from their benchmarks consistently over a long (15 year) period of time, were all led by Level 5 leaders. They were all, no doubt, ambitious people, yet they were characterized by respect for people and a virtually absent lack of self-interest. "Level 5 leaders channel their ego needs away from themselves and into the larger goal of building a great company. It's not that level 5 leaders have no ego or self-interest. Indeed, they are incredibly ambitious – but their ambition is first and foremost for the institution, not themselves."[5] They were leaders who integrated the widest perspective into their leadership, allowed the team around them to excel, and fostered the long-term contextual perspective. As one Level 5 leader said, "I want to look out from my porch at one of the great companies in the world someday and be able to say, 'I used to work there.' "

We are inspired by Jim Collins' work. He challenged us to define what practices and perspectives we can provide from our rich experience of working with leadership over several decades to develop Level 5 leaders. For that, read on!

As a final thought on the *leadership landscapes perspective*, we know that many admirable leaders use the landscapes implicitly. What is unique about our approach is that we make the practice explicit, multidimensional, and memorable through the root metaphor of landscapes as a master perspective to frame and reframe the things we do. Our purpose for making practices explicit is so that leaders can work with it and that the practice can become an embedded part of every leader's repertoire.

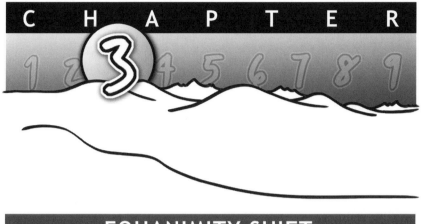

EQUANIMITY SHIFT

The Equanimity Shift to Dynamic Balance

The *equanimity shift* provides the second pillar for our work. We present a comprehensive view on an attitude of mind. It is an attitude that can be developed, nurtured, and practiced. It is the idea of *equanimity* – an approach that underpins all that we will advocate over the coming chapters. It may at first seem like an abstract notion, even a vague one, and it is in some sense elusive, but we have found it to be the key to optimal leadership.

Our first pillar, the *leadership landscapes perspective* that we touched on in the previous chapter, allows you to look across an ecology of leadership levels simultaneously, to expand your relational field of vision. It creates a context for decision making. Yet a backdrop is worthless if it is not accompanied by an attitude, a state of equanimity. A leader needs to maintain a state of, what we call, dynamic balance. While it is possible to display equanimity without the landscape practice, we have not found it possible to live the landscape practice without equanimity.

Equanimity, or dynamic balance, can be described in at least five aspects. They form – again – an integrated set, where neither is as powerful alone as when connected to the others. With the study in *Common Fire: Leading Lives of Commitment in a Complex World* [1] – a large interview-based study into leadership, concluded in 1996 – as our point of departure, we have spent the past decade working to refine our understanding of how these great leaders work. Our exploration has yielded the keystone characteristic we call "Equanimity," which we can articulate as a balancing act and one that those who have much to balance have a need to master. In common usage the term equanimity has come to mean "the quality of having an even mind." Wikipedia defines it as "the manifestation of equilibrium attained in terms of comprehension of the diverse human emotions."[2] All this is indeed what it is, but in our use as a leadership perspective it is much more.[3]

It has become clear that equanimity is something that everyone has in some measure and that the measure of a person's equanimity can be increased through practice. Like a muscle in the body, a certain level of development happens by some combination of everyday use, exertion in meeting challenging circumstances and practices directly targeted at its development. Muscles tend to work in sets. In this sense equanimity is similar to an integrated muscle set with multiple applications and ways of working.

One thing that the *Common Fire* study revealed was that leaders who sustain commitments to large-scale global and societal issues (such as public health, the environment, the prevention of deadly conflict, and poverty) displayed a high degree of equanimity in their work on the organizational, team, and personal landscapes. Or perhaps in more generic terms, those leaders that could relate their efforts to a larger perspective, which was often a commitment to add their piece to the "noble cause" they identified as deeply rooted inside them, were the ones that displayed the highest level of equanimity.

To date, many of those leaders who sustained equanimity were found in the public sector. We are witnessing, however, that great business leaders are increasingly following that track by making a connection between their own performance and a noble cause in the wider context of our (business) world.

This is not to be mistaken by leaders that transfer part of their accumulated wealth to a charity or some other "good" cause for the sake of public relations. Such motivation is – on a personal level – not sustainable. The connection to the larger perspective context comes from a generation of leaders who are connected to a wider context. Not because they are "better" people, but because this is the world they have grown up in. To borrow Thomas Friendman's terms, the world has indeed become flat.[4] Many businesses are nowadays made up from a series of subsystems that are globally spread. With that come the consciousness and the global perspective that leaders carry with them in their values and meaning. With the rise of the Internet, we only need one click to tap into suffering that goes on in some parts of the world or damage that is being done to our environment. This undoubtedly also has an impact on how modern leaders – either consciously or unconsciously – perceive their roles in society.

Peter Bakker, a young CEO of the logistics giant and EuroNext listed TNT (he took the wheel when he was 40) explains his personal commitment and involvement in fighting global problems like hunger and Aids as follows:

> We are beneficiaries of globalization. All these products have to be shipped around the world. The big problems in the world are hunger and Aids, and despite globalization we don't deal with them that well. So if we claim to be the best logistics company in the world, why can't we help?[5]

Similarly, we see a growing desire for next-generation leaders to engage in global themes. The Italian-born English educated entrepreneur Marcello Palazzi is a representative of this new breed of business leaders, who sustain their balance by creating networks and organizations that "do well" and "do good" in the world. Marcello has been the engine behind the creation of 50 organizations that have been both money producing and meaning creating for the world. He refers to the new trend as our entry into "The Civic Economy," a world where there is no split between entrepreneurs who generate wealth and those who serve the greater society. To ensure that this new breed of leaders is supported in their aspirations, in 2000 he created Business Students for social responsibility that has later become "Net Impact," a vibrant network of several thousand MBAs across the world who espouse next-generation entrepreneurship.[6]

Doing good through business is by itself not new. Also, in the past we know of many leaders in the corporate world who devoted parts of their work-life to noble causes. What we are witnessing now is an intensification of these drives for meaning. It is important to take notice of the fact that when we refer to "noble causes" it is definitely not always in the outer spectrum of world peace and such. Leaders find, and can find, noble causes in many things that are related to their commitment. One of the business leaders we will refer to later in this book is Ingvar Kamprad, the founder of IKEA, the world's biggest furniture retailer, with hundreds of stores across the globe. Known for its inexpensive, self-assembly furniture, the family-owned business claims its hefty catalogue to be the most widely read publication after the Bible.

Kamprad started doing business in his garden shed, in the early 1950s, selling watches, pens, and Christmas cards. It has been a very interesting journey from there, which eventually brought him to become – according to Forbes *The World's Richest People* – one of the wealthiest people in the world.[7] Interestingly, one of his drives for starting and growing IKEA was in fact a noble cause. In a speech for Swedish bankers in December 1976, entitled "A Furniture Dealer's Testament,"[8] Kamprad unfolded his vision for the company he was building. The speech was turned into a document, which to date is still IKEA's "bible." As he unfolds his vision, he refers to his deeper drives:

> All nations and societies in both the East and the West spend a disproportionate amount of their resources on satisfying a minority of the population. In our line of business, for example, far too many of the fine designs and new ideas are reserved for a small circle of the affluent.

To some, this may sound merely as a business vision, an insight into an untapped market, that IKEA definitely cornered over time. It surely is that as well, but to Kamprad, there was more behind it. Kamprad wanted to provide design to the non-affluent, as he believed that the company exists not just to improve people's lives, but to improve the people themselves. His message was that the self-service store design and ease of assembly of their furniture are not merely cost controls, but an opportunity for self-sufficiency.

Even though this might not be a noble cause in the league of "world peace," "saving the environment," or "fighting poverty," it is a noble cause in its own right. It is in the combination of both having a perspective on patterns in the business landscape connected to principles of equanimity, that bring out the best in our leadership.

Also, in the emerging leadership generation of today, many leaders connect both. We will meet many more in chapters to come, but it is important to realize it is not just with iconic leaders that reach well beyond most of us. Lesser known leaders often connect their motivation directly to sustained commitments that drive them forward in life. Narayana Murthy, founder of Infosys and ranked consistently as one of the leading global leaders,[9, 10] lists amongst his key features of great leadership (placed in the context of his geography) "the recognition that there are two Indias – rural and urban – and to work towards the growth of both of them."

Examples such as Kamprad, Bakker, and Murthy – and many others – show the powerful connection between the immediate business sense and more noble causes as essential to one's role as societal leader.

3.1   The pieces of equanimity

Our favorite view of equanimity reveals an integrated set of leadership attributes held together by a nucleus; each attribute is an expression of the whole characteristic. Of what then is this set of attributes comprised?

The five attributes we have found across a range of leaders are as follows:

 an *eye for possibility*;

 reframing;

 being present and *projecting presence*;

 recovery;

 enduring commitment.

We will explore these attributes in greater detail in upcoming chapters, as we explore how they relate to key themes such as vision, action, decision making, and commitment across the landscapes of leadership.

We wish to be clear that one attribute does not operate independent from the others; hence our earlier analogy to our muscular system. To deal with leadership challenges, one or more attributes will be brought to the forefront simultaneously. It is a balancing act – not that one balances the other, but all are in balance together.

On the outer edge of balance is the *eye for possibility*, which addresses the challenges and the stretching of balance. *Reframing* is closer to the center of balance; it is how you face a new situation and bring the challenge back into balance, providing coherence to the complexity. Framing the different perspectives of a situation is a way to regain balance. Yet sometimes we are pushed offbalance and brought into unforeseen situations that require us to re-balance. This is what the practice of *recovery* does; it is what you have in your leadership repertoire to regain balance after you have been tipped offbalance. *Recovery* is in that sense how we reorient towards balance. *Presence* is the face of dynamic balance. It is how dynamic balance – or equanimity – manifests itself. Certain physical acts demonstrate dynamic balance, which manifests itself in how you show up as a leader. Finally, *enduring commitment* is the underpinning

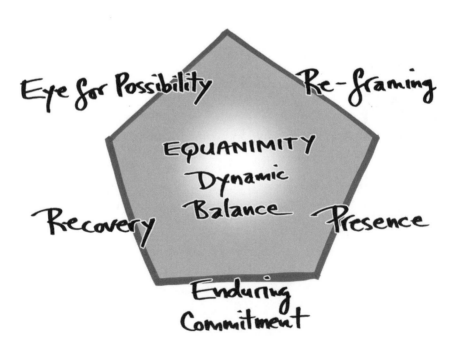

of balance; it is the gravitational force as we call it, the attribute most closely related to who we are as a person, what we stand for, and what drives us forward.

3.1.1   AN EYE FOR POSSIBILITY

Having an *eye for possibility* is the attribute of equanimity that precedes all others, as it is the equanimity attribute that is directly related to the radicality of human choice, of always having a choice. At the heart of having an *eye for possibility* is the mindset of discovery or the will to look for a third alternative in the dilemma, to know that however difficult things may get, there is always a choice.

This goes for the opportunity-seeking sense of possibility, which we typically associate with entrepreneurial leadership, against the background of continuous progress and growth. In that position, having an eye for possibility is an opportunity-scanning device, both in the development of strategic options as well as in resolving resource conflicts and other choices leaders are faced with.

Yet, it is also the mindset of realizing that, even in the most dire situations, human beings still have a choice as to how they respond. In the face of tremendous challenge, or even when facing total despair, having an *eye for possibility* captures the fundamental mindset of always having a human choice. As we see in Chapter 4, when we visit this attribute in more detail, even in the most dramatic and horrendous situations of being imprisoned and awaiting a near certain death in a concentration camp in the Second World War, Viktor Frankl[11] witnessed fellow camp prisoners who shared their bread with others, awaiting a nearly certain death of starvation. Even though they knew life was ending for them, they chose how they wanted to live toward their final moments.

An *eye for possibility* is therefore an existential choice – it is much more than seeing opportunity and acting on it (although that is certainly included as well); it is about being able to see what others miss, even in the most challenging situations. In our experience, leaders with an *eye for possibility* take others to vision and hope rather than to disorientation and despair.

3.1.2 REFRAMING

Following the *eye for possibility* comes the ability to Reframe. *Reframing*, as we see it, comes as a result of the *eye for possibility*. You cannot reframe without having an *eye for possibility*, yet the reverse is not true. So, reframing is to follow through on the ability to see possibility when others see none, by shifting the perspective and adjusting one's "sense-making frame" to the situation.

Reframing relates strongly with the readiness to face a new situation, where finding suitable frameworks for sense making is often required immediately, and, in the case of exemplary leaders, the reframing process is used repeatedly to tune themselves more acutely to the situation as it evolves. *Reframing* very often goes under the heading of "paradigm shifting", or the more popular notion of seeing the same reality through different lenses (or eyes).

To shift one's frame is often a matter of bringing background factors to the front and changing how a challenge is set against the background or context. Leaders who reframe bring different approaches to seemingly intractable situations. In the *leadership landscape perspective* it is often bringing a landscape in sight that can suddenly provide a very different perspective. One very effective technique in this model is "bumping up challenges to a higher landscape." What we mean is that seemingly intractable challenges can all of a sudden be seen from a different perspective when viewed on the higher landscape. In our leadership programs, we often entertain exercises in which people share challenges that they face today. For example, someone once described an all too familiar situation in which he had to bring about a governance change in departmental responsibilities. The challenge was not the design factor of these new responsibilities but getting the departments, and their department heads, to work together. He listed a range of issues that he was faced with, many historical, and some actually "real" issues, that one could find "valid" arguments for – systems were not aligned, risk factors were introduced, and so on. As with any change process, there is always an argument as to why it would not work. Also, he listed all the efforts he had already undertaken to get them to work together, to stimulate cooperation, to force them through a model of alignment. Nothing helped, and he was stuck with a seemingly impossible challenge.

We suggested to him to try "bumping his challenge up the landscape" and see what came out of it. Obviously he was unclear with what we suggested, so we determined first the landscape on which his challenge resided. Clearly, this was an organizational challenge he faced, with governance, responsibility, systems, and more. We challenged him to look at the issue from the next landscape up, the *industry and markets landscape.* Immediately he had to admit he had never looked at the problem from the perspective of the client. What does this challenge he was faced with mean for the client? Or from the perspective of competition – how were competitors organized to service their clients? Were they not much better facilitated to offer solutions, because they had integrated the same units? He admitted he had never taken these perspectives into account and had purely focused on *organizational landscape* factors and arguments. With the fresh perspective of the client, the competition, and other players of the next level landscape, he found new and much more powerful arguments to justify his change. Also he found renewed motivation and determination to make the change happen, as through the course of the exercises he had started to lose motivation to break through walls. Now, he saw with new eyes why the change was of pivotal importance.

The practice of reframing contrasts, of course, with the all-too-frequent leadership refrain: "If your approach is not working, do more of it, or do it harder." While this sometimes can yield results – often enough by reinforcing leaders into repeating their behavior – it is a costly leadership strategy particularly when it becomes habitual, and can yield leadership burnout, team failure, organization dysfunction, and long-term disasters.

In 2002, Numico – a Euronext-listed multinational in baby and clinical food – was on the verge of bankruptcy. The company had been successful throughout the 1990s and toward the end of the 1990s it had come to believe that their traditional markets had matured and saturated. In order to achieve its growth targets, amidst an exploding and overconfident global economy, it decided to expand and buy itself into the vitamin sector. Strategically, this seemed to be a defendable move, with vitamins being a related category to the health food business Numico already was in. So it acquired the US-based firms GNC in 1999 and Rexall Sundown in 2000.

Soon after, the acquisitions turned out to be a disaster and brought the company on its knees. Eventually, this led to the departure of their CEO, Hans van der Wielen. The new CEO who was brought in, Jan Bennink, found a company in despair. Just imagine, a once proud and successful company, situated in a small region of the world, had made global acquisitions based on their confidence that the world was at their feet. But in a matter of just three years, it had become a spectacular loser and found itself forced to sell off its new acquisitions. Bringing them back into the business with no further growth future – and if they had a future at all – it was bound by a deplorable financial state.

Jan Bennink, however, turned out to be the right man for the job at the right time. He was quick to act in restructuring the company. But more importantly, he reframed the reality of all inside Numico by simply declaring that there was tremendous growth in baby food. He shifted the paradigm from a collective self-limiting belief that there was no further growth in baby food, to a belief that this was actually a very promising category. In other words, he reframed their core assumptions. Not only was baby food a promising category again, subcategories also became promising again. So in effect, he reframed by renovating the organization's whole assumptive framework about their products, but also about their markets, the organization, and the people in it who went from being despair-laden losers to optimistic winners.

In the immediate years that followed, Numico saw a remarkable resurrection and became the darling of the stock exchange. Bennink's collective paradigm shift turned the company into a vibrant organization that started to see growth opportunities, new products, and new services, and to realize outstanding growth numbers.

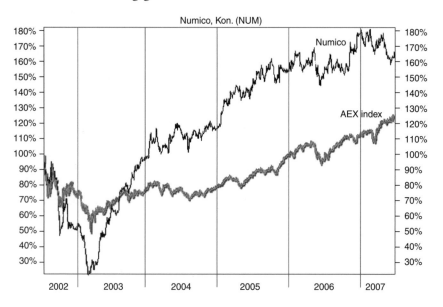

This example demonstrates the power behind a mastery of frame shifting, one more ingredient to sustain dynamic balance.

As an aside to the story of Numico, in 2007 in the eyes of the public (and the political domain) Jan Bennink became "yet another" money-greedy CEO, after it became public that, as a result of his bonus structure, he had earned over 14 million euros in 2006. Following years of public debate on exorbitant remuneration packages for top management and after the Dutch industry had applied self-regulation and had broadly accepted the "Code Tabaksblatt"* for acceptable compensation levels and structures

---

* Named after Moris Tabaksblatt, former CEO of Unilever, who headed the committee that developed the code.

to top management, this information revived the discussion on acceptable compensation levels. Interestingly, inside Numico – where one could expect the first resistance – his tremendous financial gain went uncontested, most likely because everyone enjoyed the company's resurrection and recognized Bennink as having played a key role in it.

3.1.3   BEING PRESENT AND PROJECTING PRESENCE

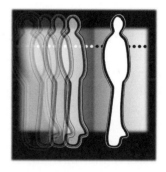

Presence is the face of dynamic balance. It is pivotal because there is no leadership without presence. You can describe the leadership role, you can call someone a leader, but there is no leader until the presence in the role shows up.

We speak of presence in terms of the influence and effect one has when walking into a room. How do leaders present themselves in their interaction with others? Is it energizing, neutral, or deflating to be in their presence? "Presencing" is also the ability to be fully present, to shift focus to where you are right now. By bringing yourself fully to a situation, you are practicing dynamic balance. The *presence* attribute of the *dynamic balance* model is therefore the crystallization of *dynamic balance*. It is the external perception of how others perceive a leader to experience and express dynamic balance.

To make the point, we draw an example from *Common Fire*[12] that provides a comprehensive basis of scientific research for our work. The dean of a graduate school, widely admired for the broad commitments and achievements that distinguished his career, reflected in an interview on significant influences in his life. An African American veteran of the Second World War, he found himself in graduate school at an Ivy League University, where he was very much a minority. There he had as his mentor a widely known and respected scholar – the jewel in the crown of that graduate faculty. The interview spoke of the many struggles he faced during that time and how he would look forward to his meetings with this professor.

You would enter his office and sit down at the appointed time and he would be deeply into his scholarship, reading, sometimes writing. Then when he turned toward you, you felt his full presence inviting you to share with him whatever you needed to communicate about your scholarly work or about other life circumstances affecting your performance. And he would listen carefully and respond constructively to all you shared. And I have made it a point to carry that forth in my own work. To come as close to that full presence as I can as often as I can.

Presence, then, is about how we show up, how we listen, how we communicate caring and coherence, and how we radiate our appearance. It is how others experience our leadership qualities.

3.1.4 RECOVERING ONESELF

Recovering is the ability to bounce back to balance when one is brought off dynamic balance. It is the recovery of equanimity or one's sense of balance in the wake of losing it in a challenging situation. It can be likened to the manner in which an athlete gains, regains, and maintains balance in the flow of performance. It is done kinesthetically, by being in tune with the body's balancing mechanism – a dance between the inner ear, body memory from training, and a flow of quick, precise decisions in the interface of the conscious and subliminal mind. So it is with the recovery of equanimity. There appears to be some kind of trigger, something akin to the inner ear in physical balance and some form of letting go of what is holding one out of balance that shifts one back into balance.

Returning to equanimity can be like facing a new situation because equanimity is either maintained or momentarily lost and then recovered. In facing a new situation there is always the possibility of being knocked askew by the force of circumstance, but returning to equanimity is always about getting back to balance – it is about recovering oneself so that one stands in confidence, performing in an optimal manner.

Our colleagues Janet Jones[13] and the late K. Bradford Brown refer to this practice as shifting one's attitudinal state – the ability to be knocked from an empowered state to survival, or even worse, impossibility, and then to bounce back to a more powerful self, the state of willingness. It can happen in a split second or in half a year, and as soon as it happens creative possibilities begin to open up, and new and powerful responses to those circumstances become possible.

3.1.5 ENDURING COMMITMENT

Finally, enduring commitment acts as a gravitational force. It draws the five aspects of equanimity into a coherent whole even as it infuses the landscape master tool with its orienting compass. In our view, enduring commitment in equanimity integrates the outcomes of the *Common Fire* study of commitment with our own subsequent and cur-  rent work with leaders. Enduring commitments develop as central themes in the tapestry of each leader's life. We draw on the material of our key experiences, hopes, and aspirations to compose our enduring commitments. It requires developing, reworking, and refining commitments as we go on in life.

While the process of sustaining commitments is mostly implicit, most of us can recall moments in our lives when our enduring commitments helped us find our way during critical forks in the road. Enduring commitments can express themselves as episodes in a deeper intent of a particular life or project at hand. Acting on our deep intent propels us to address a series of more immediate questions of intent. What horizons are you working toward? What landscapes are you engaging in this work? How clearly are you bringing your vision to life and enrolling others in sharing it? Our responses are most robust and enliven us with the deepest meaning and purpose when we sense in them the underpinning of enduring commitment.

One of the highly talented people we work with in our leadership journeys is David Pearl of the London-based David Pearl Group.[14] He helps leaders to (re-)discover their deep intent to draw on powerful energies for their life projects. Using lessons and experiences from the world of performing arts, David Pearl shows leaders how to find, connect, and use the awareness of deep intent to business performance in a day-to-day setting. The experience of discovering one's deep intent is often regarded upon by the leaders we work with as one of the most satisfying, helpful, and meaningful experiences in their leadership journey. It quite often leads to breakthrough moments in how they see themselves in relationship to the *leadership landscapes* – whether that is how they perceive their own leadership style (*individual landscape*), how they show up with their team (*team landscape*), how they deal with the organizational challenges, for example a reorganization (*organization landscape*), how they redefine what is important in the industry landscape of clients, competitors, and stakeholders (*industry landscape*), or how they relate to the challenges of the wider world we all live in (Macro Business Landscape).

To illustrate how enduring commitments have a tremendously significant and meaningful – and eventually also commercially satisfying – role in a leader's life, we close this quick tour on Equanimity, which we explore in further detail in upcoming chapters, with a story drawn from Michael Useem's wonderful book *Leadership Moments*.[15] It is a story about Dr. Roy Vagelos, a physician and biochemist at Merck & Company, one of the United States' leading pharmaceutical firms.

In the mid-1970s, Dr. Vagelos was senior vice president of research and headed a team of extraordinarily talented scientists. In the light of ending patent protection on some very successful drugs, the team was encouraged as well as pressured to come up with new blockbusters for Merck. A fortune was invested to facilitate the scientists in their search. Under Roy Vagelos's direction, the lab consumed almost a billion dollars between 1975 and 1978, much of it going to highly paid scientists who were encouraged to pursue their instincts, publish their results, and view their studies as a means of mitigating human suffering.

Fortunately enough, during their very rigorous search, they discovered a naturally occurring microbe that showed very interesting results on their laboratory mice. The science team, headed by William Campbell, followed the track and discovered in 1978 that the drug they were developing – by now called Ivermectin – could quite possibly lead to a cure for river blindness. River blindness was a disease with devastating effect that had infected millions of people, mainly in Africa, but also in Latin America. It was caused by a parasite worm that gradually could lead to blindness. The World Health Organization had calculated that by the 1970s, 85 million people were at risk, with millions already suffering from it directly.

Upon their initial findings and indications in 1977, Campbell reported it back to Vagelos, who encouraged him to keep following the track. And in 1979, having collected the scientific evidence needed, they were ready to present their findings to the decision-making committee, chaired by Vagelos. On paper, the case had the odds against it: the potential customer base consisted of the world's most impoverished people, antiparasitic drugs were known to fail, and there was a significant chance that side effects on human application would be reported, which would have a devastating effect on the animal application (which was another application area they were thinking of). Yet, despite serious counter pressure, Vagelos forced the project to continue, and by 1980, Vagelos approved the first clinical trials in West Africa. The experimental results were, despite skepticism from a range of experts, more than promising and showed that only a small amount of Ivermectin had sustained impact on worm count with the human patients. The scientific community was not buying it however, and their representatives warned in the *Lancet*, the leading British medical journal, to not be overoptimistic. Merck continued its trials over 1983–1986, fine-tuning the medication and increasing the trial population, which continued to confirm their findings. With just one or two pills a year, river blindness could be brought to a halt for most of the investigated patients.

By 1987, Roy Vagelos had further moved up the ranks, and had now become the CEO of Merck. In contrast to his previous roles, he now also had to take the interest of other stakeholders into account, when he was faced with the decision to push for commercial approval in 1987. This was not an easy decision, as it was obvious at that moment that there was not any immediate commercial success at the horizon. Production costs alone were very likely not to be recovered by sales – in addition, there was a big cost factor in distributing the drug, as most of the patients lived in places that were very hard to reach. To overcome having to carry all the financial burden and risks, Vagelos approached the government agencies that should have an interest in having the drug produced and distributed into these very poor areas. Yet, over and over again, he did not get any support. Even the former U.S. Secretary of State Henry Kissinger got involved, opening doors in all directions, but still the results remained the same.

As Vagelos was making his decision to continue to support the drug, in spite of all the resistance, he chose in the end to give it away to all who need it and decided to organize and fund the distribution to the remote areas. This was a risky decision to make, as it was not apparent to everyone that this was in the shareholders's interests. Interestingly, to justify his decision, Vagelos could tap into the deeply rooted history of Merck, a company whose history dates back to 1668. The deeply rooted culture in the company had always been to put patients first and the company and shareholders second. As Vagelos explained "Sometimes in your life you've got to take a leadership position and make a decision."

Roy Vagelos' story is an illustration of enduring commitment on two levels. At the organization's landscape, the corporate culture within Merck allowed Vagelos to make the decisions he made, which might or would have been challenged in many other organizations. In the Merck culture to truly "put patients first," Vagelos found the support to continue to spend money on creation and production of a drug with very little commercial viability from the start. Also, on the individual landscape, it is Vagelos' leadership, which is driven by his enduring commitment to do good, that helped him make and defend his decisions in the face of resistance and complete lack of support.

To complete the story, in the end the sustained efforts resulted in several commercial successes. Applications in the agricultural domain would become the world's leading health care product for animals, and Merck's second biggest money maker ever (in 1997, revenue from the drug was near US $1 billion). Less quantitative, but equally valuable, indirect outcomes were also acknowledged, such as the confirmation of Merck's culture to put the patient first, which became an important factor in its continuation to attract world-class scientific talent.

3.2 The whole of equanimity

This brings us back to our starting point. Earlier we described equanimity as an integrated set of attributes held together by a nucleus. We see the nucleus as the balancing point of the mind, developed over years of practice. Equanimity is often defined in a manner that comes close to "even-mindedness." We prefer a more robust but compatible expression – dynamic balance – the sense of maintaining balance in the flow of thought, action, and change, triggering a return to balance when it has been disrupted.

Leaders who sustain enduring commitments and keep themselves robust and flexible in facing an uncertain, changing world of multiple landscapes, have either learned how to trigger their own rebalancing as a reflex or have learned to trigger rebalancing more consciously through means they can access when they sense the loss of balance. There are a number of means for doing this and the best advice may be to locate the triggers for rebalancing that one uses naturally and learn to use them more consciously.

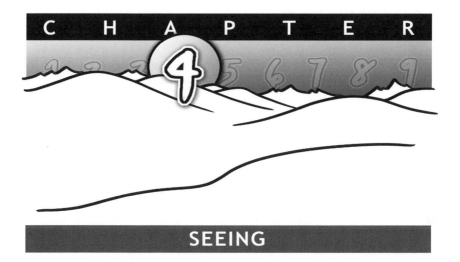

CHAPTER 4

SEEING

Leadership Seeing: How We Enact an Eye for Possibility and Reframe

One of our colleagues, Rob-Jan de Jong, a strategist, whose work is around engaging leaders to embrace the future,[1] sometimes starts his leadership seminars with the question "What is the one word used in every definition of leadership?" The first reaction is consistently "vision." Indeed, we do associate leadership very strongly with the concept of creating, maintaining, and sharing a vision. Yet, when he asks a follow-up question to his groups of senior leaders, querying them on "who feels that they have a vision (e.g. about where their industry is going)?", hardly anyone raises their hand.

As he further explores this paradox, and why it is that we all acknowledge that vision and leadership are closely linked theoretically but not practically, he finds that a vital quality to create an effective and inspiring vision is imagination. Yet imagination is something we are encouraged to unlearn by our rational upbringing and the incentive systems we adopt and adhere to as we move up in the corporate world. But in order to develop and maintain a powerful vision, one that faces, reframes, and deals with the inherent uncertainties of the future, imagination is an essential and pivotal skill. Yet, it is clearly an undervalued quality in boardrooms today.

Through the ages, since the times of the Delphi oracle, one of the most highly prized qualities of leaders has been "vision." Why, then, do we not run an MBA class: "Visioning 101" or "Essentials of Visioning"? And why has the idea of having a vision been discounted in the face of short-term reactionary and opportunistic moves?

One reason is that we see vision as an ideal rather than as a context in which we get things done. One could say that anything that becomes an ideal becomes twice as hard to achieve, however inspiring it may be.

Yet, if we establish a vision as the context to guide our actions, the *raison d'être* of our every move, then we can scale our efforts back to more manageable terms and focus on developing the qualities we need to support our actions toward that vision, no matter how complex and changing the conditions we face.

Two powerful qualities of our *equanimity shift*, above all others, will keep us on the path as leaders who commit to enact a vision: sustaining an *eye for possibility* and *reframing* our thinking, offering a mindset and assumptions we need in the face of new, competing information.

4.1   Eye for Possibility

> *Most people see things as they are and wonder why,*
> *I see things that never were and say, why not?*
> Robert Kennedy

The *eye for possibility* stands behind such familiar expressions as finding the silver lining in the cloud and seeing the glass presented as half empty also as half full. Not to be mistaken for rose-colored glasses, the *eye for possibility* appraises how the glass may be both full and empty even as it searches for the way forward when the path appears to be blocked. Moreover the *eye for possibility* casts light illuminating familiar patterns afresh, revealing new options and alternative pathways to be considered.

A leader's capacity to have an *eye for possibility* hinges on sustaining a mindset that sees a way forward, whether tapping into an opportunity (the positive perspective) or seeing a way out (the more challenging perspective). In the positive perspective, entrepreneurial context is the mindset of constant curiosity and having an obsession with the future and the opportunities it represents.

Essential in the way we see the *eye for possibility* is that it consciously engages with one of our most powerful human qualities, our imagination. In a philosophical sense, it is the most existential attribute in our model. The wondering eye is the eye of imagination.

But just as every entrepreneur carries stories of grasped opportunities, behind those same entrepreneurs are always stories where all seemed to fail, where seemingly impossible barriers had to be overcome or all would go up in smoke. It is therefore also the moments of challenge and despair that mark the leader's *eye for possibility*. We will draw out both perspectives in this chapter, the opportunistic eye, as well as the survivor's eye, as they are part of the same phenomenon, an *eye for possibility*.

In the autobiographical account of the psychological degradation experienced daily in a Nazi concentration camp, psychiatrist Viktor Frankl related how he discovered the elemental nature of free will. He observed that "even in such terrible conditions of psychic and physical stress" exists "the last of human freedoms – to choose one's attitude in any given set of circumstances, to choose one's own way."[2]

In the second half of this remarkable book which speaks to people today after more than half a century, Frankl describes an approach that emerged for him for addressing despair out of the ashes of the concentration camp. To paraphrase his work, we must not deny the situation in which we find ourselves, but rather we must choose the manner in which to bear the burden at hand. Only in this way do we make meaningful the questions life asks of us. At the same time, to be able to choose our path, even in the most desperate circumstances, a presence of mind is required, an equanimity, an ability to stay balanced in the face of anything that comes your way.

Having eventually survived the concentration camp, he established himself as a psychiatrist again in the years following the Second World War. Bringing his own horrendous experiences to his practice with the aim of serving others, he told the story[3] of an older professional man who came to his psychiatric office one day. "Dr. Frankl," he announced, "[S]ince the death of my wife, I am unable to get on with my life. I loved her so deeply and my heart is broken from losing her." He found the man in complete despair of having lost the person he loved most and facing a reality in which he no longer could or wanted to live. It was a man who had lost all that he believed was worth living for.

Drawing upon his own experiences of having lived in a situation of total despair and loss of perspective, Frankl's approach to help this man through this seemingly impossible barrier was to engage with the art of inquiry. His ambition was to ask the question that would trigger his patient's shift from despair to possibility. Frankl had learned that providing a way for people to make new meaning out of their suffering was an important key to pulling people out of immense lowpoints in their lives.

As he began to work with the man, Frankl recounts in his book, he asked him at some point "what if you had died first, and left her to grieve?". It turned out to be the trigger question Frankl was looking for. The patient, as he considered this question, started to see a new possibility. Indeed, he realized, by surviving his wife and bearing the pain of her loss, he could act out of love for her, knowing that by surviving her, he had spared her the pain of losing him and of having to get on with her life. The despair lifted as he shifted to this new possibility.

Victor Frankl's practice demonstrates the power of sustaining an *eye for possibility*. Naturally, people are not always driven to despair, yet often it is at the low points in our lives, or in business cycles, that having and sustaining an *eye for possibility* becomes pivotal to leadership. It is the person who, in the face of enormous, sometimes unbearable challenges, successfully maintains an *eye for possibility*, who turns a threat into an opportunity, a betrayal into a chess game, or a heavy situation into an exciting challenge.

4.2   Sharpening an Eye for Possibility

As we expressed before, the *eye for possibility* is the most existential attribute of the dynamic balance model. It reflects the state of mind of having a wondering eye, being curious, discovering, finding a way how the different elements configure together, finding a way out, and being alert to change.

As it encompasses all that – and because of its existential nature – it is an inherent leadership attitude, a mindset that must be deeply rooted in a leader. It is therefore certainly not a "feature" that can be outsourced to anyone else – not a junior, not a planning or strategy department. Surely, others can help and support the ongoing development and maintenance of one's *eye for possibility*, but having an *eye for possibility* is inherent to great leadership. No form of delegation or externalization can be applied to create a mindset of curiosity. In that sense, as a leader, one must be aware of its essential requirement and its impact on how leadership is perceived.

There is no single path to follow to create an *eye for possibility*. It is really a mindset, an attitude, and a behavior. Toward this end we offer a number of exercises to sharpen an *eye for possibility*. These practices can easily be adopted in daily lives and generally require on-going practice to master. Give them a try. They are simple and straightforward:

▶ One approach is to start by noticing things, noticing how things shape what is around you, how you perceive them, and how they are being perceived by others. As obvious as it sounds, very often we do not practice our perception in our busy daily lives. Overfull agendas force us through the day, and stop us from truly noticing things. But only when we master ourselves in becoming conscious of the things around us – how we ourselves, as well as our family, colleagues, and others behave and respond to reality, will we be able to notice changes that take place. Change rarely happens very suddenly, but is usually a hardly noticeable gradual process. It is those that have logged how things were, that are the earliest to notice how things have changed.

▶ Another practice to engage in is to consciously take a moment to reflect. In Chapter 8 we will go in detail on how reflection can work for you, and how to powerfully reflect, yet at this stage we want to establish that reflecting serves to sharpen our *eye for possibility*.

▶ A third approach is to listen in a more radical way. Deep listening to another's perspective is as enriching as trying to create an answer yourself. Often when we listen, we fall back into judgment mode, and therefore do not hear what is actually being communicated. We listen to what we want to hear, or do not want to hear, and respond to it. By truly listening we construct mental images that support gaining new insights and seeing new possibilities. It is not required that you agree with everything you listen to; but the experience of allowing yourself to listen deeply helps you – through a conscious action – to create your own mental images and shape your sense of possibility. Simply put, this works because to listen deeply, you must withhold judgment, and engage your curiosity. As this becomes your mental start point in the conversation, it will prevent you from making judgments and allow yourself to truly contemplate, learn, and gather the information that is being provided to you.

▶ Our final approach to sustaining an *eye for possibility* is to build conversational partnerships with others who broaden and deepen one's perspectives. Particularly enriching are conversational partners from significantly different disciplines, such as from the arts, or from fundamentally different industries. Richard Feinman, the Nobel Prize winning physicist made a point of seeking out experiences with artists to broaden his physicist's eye. Engaging in conversational partnerships, or coaching relationships, with individuals that provide different insights and reflections, is a powerful way of sharpening your *eye for possibility*. As an aside, mastering deep listening, the previous approach, is conditional to engaging powerfully in conversational partnerships. You will only be able to build up meaningful conversational partnerships if you master the art of deep listening.

In Chapter 8 we will deepen some of these approaches that work for you in sharpening the equanimity attributes and in particular the *eye for possibility*.

4.3 The art of reframing

Reframing is a powerful complementary skill to cultivate with an *eye for possibility*. *Reframing* is the art of seeing the same reality through different eyes. By developing and exercising an *eye for possibility* one is able to reframe assumptions and thinking. On the other hand, one can have an *eye for possibility*, yet not be able to reframe. In that case, we will notice something brought to us by our wondering eye, but it will either reinforce our current frame (which is entirely possible if the information does not require you to reframe) or – and this is more troublesome – we will simply file it away. When we simply file information that does not fit in our current frame of assumptions, it does nothing to challenge our "sense-making frame." *Reframing* is thus the ability to use new information and allowing one's self to reframe perspective on a changed reality.

Reframing is a consistent attitude and practice that understands that a particular perspective on a matter, even if it is the popular belief, is just one perspective, one lens on reality that can be viewed through many. As human beings, we often fixate our perspectives in a way that is not very flexible. We have a tendency to color our perspective, for instance, with rules, limitations, constraints, self-limiting beliefs, or other fixations. Unfortunately when we are not aware of this colored picture, our perspective is limited.[4]

The conscious practice of reframing is cultivated by great leaders. They have the ability to change perspectives, to change the frame through which they see themselves, as well as an ability to change the reality of those they lead. In our earlier example in Chapter 3, Jan Bennink, the CEO of Numico, reframed the organization's collective perspective by dismissing their "self-limiting" belief that their product range did not have any future growth. This belief represented the collective mindset when he entered the company in 2002, as a result of believed saturated traditional markets and highly unsuccessful entries into new markets. *Reframing* in that sense is also about providing a different perspective, usually a positive and inspiring one, and sometimes a usefully disconfirming one.

It should be clear by now that reframing is a practice that both challenges conventional wisdom to create new visions and inspires others to reconsider long held beliefs. A powerful vision built on reconsidered and reframed ideas taps into our imagination and sheds a directional light on the path forward. It often has the power to inspire. Leaders use vision to express their different – and inspiring – perspective on reality to stir imagination and create forward momentum. Those who can reframe are able to break through the walls of conventional thinking, and can energize teams and organizations.

Blue Ocean Strategy,[5] the international bestseller of Chan Kim and Renee Mauborgne, describes the power that reframing exerts on an industry landscape. The book is devoted to showing that leading companies do not succeed by battling competitors – creating bloody "red oceans" – but by creating "blue oceans" of uncontested market space, ripe for growth. They dub it "value innovation," powerful leaps in value created for both the company and its buyers, rendering rivals obsolete, and unleashing new demand. These strategic moves are sometimes a result of seeing completely new things on the horizon, but more often it is in seeing the same reality through different eyes that provides the strategic insights. In our words, the art of reframing is the leader's skill to unleash creativity and uncover opportunities.

> To set a company on a strong, profitable growth trajectory in the face of these industry conditions, it won't work to benchmark competitors and try to outcompete them by offering a little more for a little less. Such a strategy may nudge sales up but will hardly drive a company to open up uncontested market space. Nor is conducting extensive customer research the path to blue oceans. [...] And what customers typically want "more" of are those product and service features that the industry currently offers.
>
> To fundamentally shift the strategy canvas of an industry, you must begin by reorienting your strategic focus from competitors to alternatives, and from customers to non-customers of the industry. To pursue both value and cost, you should resist the old logic of benchmarking competitors in the existing field and choosing between differentiation and cost leadership. As you shift your strategic focus from current

competition to alternatives and non-customers, you gain insight into how to redefine the problem the industry focuses on and thereby reconstruct buyer value elements that reside across industry boundaries.

Kim and Mauborgne clearly propose a way of seeing an industry that requires leaders to develop their reframing skills. They reframe our assumptions about traditional approaches such as benchmarking against existing competition, to focus our attention on alternatives and non-customers. This is "reframing at work" on an industry landscape.

Another wonderful illustration of extremely powerful reframing comes from Silvia Lagnado, Global Brand Director for Unilever who led Dove's Campaign for Real Beauty. The campaign caused a shockwave in the field of advertising and branding, leaving many experts to rethink their assumptions about what makes a powerful brand. As one of the researchers involved in the 2004 global research, puts it: "For too long beauty has been defined by narrow, stifling stereotypes, you've told us it's time to change all that. We agree. Because we believe real beauty comes in many shapes, sizes and ages."[6]

Dove's Campaign for Real Beauty is a refreshingly different approach to marketing and provision of beauty products. It's an applied example of challenging a conventional perspective of marketing beauty products that was aimed at both sociocultural change *and* commercial success.

Silvia Lagnado joined Unilever's marketing department in her native Brazil in 1987. Despite her uncommon background – she holds a civil engineering degree – she rapidly moved through the ranks of marketing, working on and holding responsibility for several branding campaigns. As she stepped up to a global role as global brand director in 2002, there was only one brand she was interested in working on: Dove. The brand, which at that stage consisted primarily of moisturizers, subsequently became a deodorant brand, stretched into shampoos and has now crossed a lot of other categories, while at the same time providing a landmark challenge on how beauty is to be portrayed.

Silvia Lagnado's different perspective on beauty had not appeared to her at the very start of her job. It goes to show that a reframed reality is usually not a starting point, but it is part of a process of ongoing sense making, which could eventually lead to the key insight, the reframed reality. As she started her job building the Dove brand, she went through a long series of meetings and discussions about the brand strategy. Being able to fall back on Unilever's extensive knowledge of branding, and having all the experts available to discuss, she worked herself through the numerous sessions of well-intended expert advice. At some point, during a break, she reflected with some colleagues on how she felt about all this.

In honesty, she responded that she thought it was actually quite bizarre how beauty was defined in our society. She witnessed and experienced the – conventional – marketing rules that beauty must be portrayed by beautiful and happy people, that live up to physical attributes we associate with beauty. But "when I look at my own daughter, and see the unhappiness and degrading effect this beauty ideal has on that generation, I sometimes wonder why we so desperately must uphold that image of beauty." Her reframing of reality, the notion that there was another way to see the "rules of beauty," that was not conventional, but just as much a reality as the one forced upon us, initiated the start of one of the most successful branding campaigns in beauty products.

As she came to realize what she had just expressed, and encouraged by her colleagues to explore her thoughts further, she experienced how deep this actually connected to a commitment she wanted to stand for. Silvia Lagnado had discovered a motivation that became the inner drive behind her work, which started her path that eventually led to The Campaign for Real Beauty.

The Campaign for Real Beauty arose from a ten-country study called "The Real Truth about Beauty," which Dove conducted with Harvard University and the London School of Economics in 2004. Based on the responses from over 3200 women, the study set out to learn about women's views on their own beauty. Using rigorous academic and polling research[7] the group revealed that of the 3200 women surveyed in ten countries, only a small minority saw themselves as above average in appearance and only 2 percent claim to be beautiful. Only 9 percent even considered themselves attractive.

The campaign's mission therefore became to expand and challenge society's rigid definition of beauty. The first phase did just that, by using a series of outdoor billboards and print ads that featured non-traditional beauties and challenging viewers to visit a website and vote on each image – wrinkled or wonderful, fat or fit, freckled or fabulous.

The campaign received a mixed reception. Some saw it to be part of a wider social movement, the so-called beauty backlash. Others were even more skeptical: "As a woman, I feel good about the Dove ads, but as a marketer, I still have to know; where's the money?" said Mary Lou Quinlan, from Just Ask a Woman, a marketing consultancy. "Using the average person won't sell anything" says Gerald Celente, director and founder of Trends Research Institute, a consultancy.

The purpose of advertising is to create desire beyond what the product can actually deliver. Do you want to see the floppy Big Mac that the fast food worker actually packages up and hands to you, or the perfect airbrushed billboard version? People are living lives of desperation; they don't want to be themselves.

Gerald Celente may have been critical of the ads themselves but he has been forced to acknowledge that the campaign has broken through the "mindless clutter" of today's media. The Dove campaign has had a much bigger impact than anything similar done before.

By reframing the world as she saw it, and overcoming the conventional backlashes that any new angle to reality is likely to encounter, Silvia Lagnado has created a landmark example of the power of reframing. Not only had she established herself as a leader – and thought leader – in achieving a more genuine and honest look towards real beauty, but she has also managed to stand tall against the resistant conventional patterns that are in place and that strongly work against reframing.[8]

The story of Dove is also a story of commercial success, which makes this illustration even more powerful. When the campaign was launched in the United Kingdom, revenues went up 700 per cent in the first year. As the commercial success might give rise to the thought that that would be all that matters to Dove, and their marketing teams, this is countered by Dove's continued and sustained effort into the campaign. Followed up by further academic research in the following years, the creation of the Dove Self Esteem Fund and Dove's sustained dedication to challenge the rules around beauty, and look at beauty from within, embodies a relationship with a more noble cause, besides being commercially successful. Interestingly in this respect, as other advertisers started to witness the success of the Dove campaign, it was soon followed and copied by others. Yet their efforts failed, and their attempts of trying to copy a competitor's strategy appeared futile, simply because the campaign came from Dove's heart, not theirs.

4.4   Key principles of reframing

We boil down the art of reframing to two key principles that must be in place to optimize the circumstances of powerful reframing to take place. These principles work at every landscape, whether it is reframing one's individual perspective or reframing the rules of the game in your business, or even the macro-business landscape.

Reframing is in essence a creative process which cannot be forced upon an individual or organization. We cannot provide a recipe to reframe, but we can maximize the circumstances in which powerful reframing is most likely to occur. Viewed from a negative angle, when these principles are absent – in an individual or in an organization – the risks (and costs) of remaining stuck in a paradigm that is no longer in line with reality are much higher. This is later illustrated in this chapter by the story of Wal-Mart, which lost US $1 billion by not adhering to one of these principles.

The key principles for effective reframing are as follows:

▶ honoring diversity
▶ a safe space to create.

4.4.1   KEY PRINCIPLE 1: HONORING DIVERSITY

One of the characteristics of diversity – in science, in technology, in biology, in culture, in software, or in children – is that the underlying programming tends to be open source, or connected in all directions.

George Dyson, Infinite in Three Directions:
In Praise of Open Thinking (2006)

Upon finishing their education, many young people pack their backpacks and travel the planet for a while. Some are drawn to the less common places in Asia, South America, and Africa, and meet a wide variety of different perspectives on how people live and experience their lives. These perspectives range from down to earth day-to-day activities such as eating, transporting, and transacting to more refined experiences such as cultural interactions and religious beliefs. And when they are lucky, they get a chance to spend some in-depth time with some of the locals and experience their lives, their routines, their behaviors, and their values.

When I ask my son[9] what he learned on his trip to Ecuador, it was the new perspectives that opened him to seeing the same reality with different eyes. And in particular, the reality of the world he returned to. It was the little things such as seeing the queue at the post office in a new perspective, and seeing the fridge not being stocked up, and it was the big things, such as seeing political and social themes differently. That is what diversity of perspectives does for us; it enriches the frame through which we approach reality with our ability to see that same reality differently.

Reframing is not about seeing new lands, but seeing the current lands with new eyes. The practice of engaging diversity is all about being able to open our minds to people, cultures, prospects, and opportunities. By engaging multilevels of perspective through our landscapes, we are discovering fresh insights and experiences. This is how we see across landscapes – "the new map" which must be (to use Dyson's term that heads this section) connected in all directions.

It is important to take notice of the fact that we do not see diversity in the – often seen – limited sense of gender-related perspectives. And we do not weigh diversity in merely cultural or ethnic terms. We see gender and ethnic diversity as part of diversity from a wider perspective. It includes differences among development, production, marketing, and sales in traditional industries, among economic, technical, and psychological lenses, the difference between temperament and talents, differences in value orientation, religion, and culture, differences in level and content of experience, and differences in generation and life span. Ultimately, diversity means being connected in webs of relationship that extend in all directions. Diversity is mostly about being truly open minded and generous, while taking multiple perspectives into consideration. Engaging with diversity is about allowing your own assumptions to be challenged by those perspectives. If one can cultivate ways to encourage diversity, reframing assumptions becomes a natural next step.

However, as writer and philosopher Ken Wilber puts it: "We don't just need a new map; we need ways to change the mapmaker."[10] Changing the mapmaker means remembering there is no room for simple assumptions and easy answers. What you need to know to engage with diversity is three simple facts:

1. start by presuming that what you know is not always useful or very useful any more;
2. then accept that there is no longer "one right way" (and never was); and
3. finally be clear that you will need to cultivate your own diverse networks and your own team to reflect a range of skills and perspectives for the journey (this is not a package holiday).

4.4.1.1   The explorer mentality

Engaging diversity was clearly key to Roald Amundsen's achievements in his groundbreaking polar explorations, as we will see in our historical illustration of landscapes and equanimity in Chapter 9. From examining his experiences, it's easy to see how an ability to engage diversity can have a revelatory impact on an organization's success. Where John Franklin – another explorer who was unsuccessful in finding the Northern Passage that Amundsen uncovered – saw frozen tundra and arctic wasteland, to Amundsen's reframing mind, a cornucopia of fresh food was revealed each day. He practiced open thinking, connected in all directions. Five hundred years of European failures had been overcome by someone at last able to be genuinely aware of his situation and to anticipate the scenarios he would encounter. His capacity to engage with the diversity of the environment and the native people he encountered, were essential to his survival.

Amundsen's lessons on diversity exhibit each of the three lessons we have outlined. He operated with a great degree of flexibility and range, having already surveyed all his options over a long period of time. He realized there was no single approach that must be obeyed. He scrapped the preconceptions on which previous expeditions had been based. He created his own team, which he coordinated with complete independence. He followed the maxim of his inspirational predecessor Fridtjof Nansen[11] who said: "Walk in no man's footsteps."

A more contemporary individual, who exhibited what we might call *explicit diversity* in the selection of his team, is polar explorer Robert Swan. In 1986, along with companions Roger Mear and Gareth Wood, Swan arrived at the South Pole after traveling 883 miles without radios or assistance of any kind. Three years later on the May 14, 1989, Swan successfully reached the North Pole and so became the first person to have walked to both poles. As he says of his own leadership experience, the lessons are simple: "Information is power. Diversity is strength. Complacency is death."

4.4.1.2   Team diversity

To achieve his Antarctic mission he handpicked a team of people with different but complementary skills to travel together to the South Pole. He included a Japanese scientist who could read the weather and a doctor that needed no tools. A crack team demonstrating explicit diversity was handpicked to be as flexible in their expertise as possible. Reflecting on his mission, he explained that as they set into their journey he realized that they all had disgusting personal habits. One suffered from extreme flatulence, one slurped noodles whilst another coughed incessantly. And to top it off, they all had egos the size of Mount Fuji.

As Swan tells this story to an expectant audience and they laugh, he pauses and says, "the point is however: 'If I'd taken my friends, I'd have died.'" It wasn't important that they all got along, it was important that they got the job done. And get the job done they did. In fact, they arrived at the South Pole five days ahead of schedule. Too often we take account of comfortable sociability rather than concentrate on the skills needed for an optimal team mix.

Swan's experience in the Antarctic completely changed his view of the world in a most unexpected way. He realized that the habitat and atmosphere had completely altered since Scott's expedition because of ozone depletion. What had been a scientific expedition and an effort to reclaim a piece of cultural and national heritage turned into a personal revelation about the state of the planet.

"What happened to us on that journey changed our lives completely," Swan says. "My eyes changed colour. They used to be dark blue, and now they're light blue, and looking at bright lights is quite difficult for me. Our faces just blistered out, and our skin continued to peel right off our faces for months."

"We had not read about that sort of thing happening in the history books," he said. "Then, when we got home, we were told that we had spent 70 days walking under this thing called a hole in the ozone layer. I'd never heard of it. But when you've experienced it firsthand – when you've had your face torched off – you take the information more seriously than you otherwise might."

By exposing himself to a unique experience, by being open to change and by engaging diversity, Swan's life and – literally – his vision of the world was changed fundamentally.

On his next trip to the North Pole his team almost drowned when the temperature rose – from −30 degrees Celsius to −5 degrees (from −22 degrees Fahrenheit to +23 degrees) – and the ice cap began to melt beneath the explorers' very feet. Swan and his team were 700 miles away from land. "It's supposed to melt in August, and this was in April." he said. "Never in recorded Arctic history had the ice cap melted in April. Obviously, that was another sign of environmental change. But at the time, our problem was how to stay alive, because we were beyond rescue of any type."

If Swan's handpicked team is a great example of what we are saying about gathering a diverse group, the land literally melting beneath their feet could not be a more explicit example of our lesson that "you need to start by presuming that what you know is not very useful any more."

Swan and his team survived due to ingenuity and their ability to act with flexibility and in no small part because of the make-up of the team. But this diversity was itself limited as Swan would controversially point out to the Explorers Club in New York in 1987. Swan said: "I've taken your Explorers Club flag to the South Pole, I'm taking it to the North Pole, it's been to the top of Mount Everest – it's been everywhere, but when did it last visit Harlem? And I notice that there aren't too many black faces in the audience."

It was a provocative and telling point to the group that had supported and funded Swan's efforts in the past. But his words acted as a spur for the Explorer's Club and Swan to do something about it.[12] There is no point in having a limited, closed, or token show of diversity. To be truly effective you must be, as George Dyson says, "open in all directions."

By looking at the story of exploration itself we are coming across new tools that are vital in the leadership challenge and presenting them back to you.

Let us explore that explorer mentality remembering Jorge Luis Borges' statement that: "Between the traditional and the new, or between order and adventure, there is no real opposition; and what we call tradition today is a knit work of centuries of adventure."

4.4.1.3 Failing diversity

As a counterpoint to these examples of people working with an expansive notion of diversity it is worth looking at a recent example of a corporate failure to engage diversity. Our example is the largest employer in the world after the Chinese Army, the retailer Wal-Mart.

The Arkansas-based company that has been such a huge commercial success in the United States (it is the world's largest retailer) has had to pull out of Germany at an estimated cost of around US $1 billion. The withdrawal is a blow to Wal-Mart's overseas ambitions, an area of increasing importance as it seeks new sources of sales growth.

In May 2006, the company announced it was to sell its 16 outlets in South Korea and exit the country. In the United Kingdom also the company has faced difficulties with its subsidiary ASDA, which it bought in 1999. A threatened strike by the GMB in July 2006 brought about significant concessions from the company allowing union access to ASDA depots for the first time. The company faces its critics at home as well with a documentary *Wal-Mart: the High Cost of Low Price* focusing on the company's less savoury practices and even a Democratic Party senator, Byron Dorgan of North Dakota publishing a book, *Take This Job and Ship It*. In it he argued that the giant retailer's out-of-town stores destroy communities by affecting the local economy.

Wal-Mart's overseas failure can to a great extent be seen as a textbook case of a company failing to engage diversity. It looks increasingly like an inflexible and one-dimensional giant unable to operate in new and changing circumstances.

But, as the Economist magazine reported, Wal-Mart's failure was predicted by academics in Bremen University three years before it actually happened. In 2003, they published a study titled: "Why did Wal-Mart fail in Germany." As the Economist put it, "... three years later the news finally reached Bentonville, Arkansas."[13]

Before that, in 2000, Metro's chief executive, Hans-Joachim Koerber, predicted that Wal-Mart would not succeed. "The company's culture does not travel, and Wal-Mart does not understand the German customer," he said. Metro has now taken over the 85 stores Wal-Mart has been forced to sell. The reasons for Wal-Mart's failure would seem to rest on a handful of critical cultural mistakes and misunderstandings that point to a total failure to embrace diversity by the American company.

Germans more than Americans tend to shop locally and more often, even if shopping "locally" may mean local discount stores like Lidl and Aldi; so their shopping culture is quite different. German shoppers tend to like to bag things themselves into reusable carriers and are unlikely to drive a few extra miles to save a euro. Most of Wal-Mart's stores were in their traditional "out-of-town" locations.

Thus, the service culture at the till and the cheaper (for Wal-Mart) location of the stores, which were an integral part of the Wal-Mart shopping experience and their previous success, were, in this context, redundant elements that actually worked against the retailer. It was the start of a catalogue of missed opportunities and failure to respond to new cultural circumstances.

While Wal-Mart's retail culture forced checkout clerks to smile at customers, this was often misconstrued in Germany, where smiles tend to occur naturally between friends and not often between people you don't know. Research shows some shoppers misinterpreted the grins of shop assistants as invitations to unwanted social interaction.

But if smiling and flirting was compulsory between workers and shoppers, it was banned among staff. Another cultural collision here as many shop workers are used to meeting in the workplace and you often find husband and wife teams working in the same stores. Wal-Mart's ban on sexual relations between staff was overturned in the German courts a year after it had been put in place but it is another key indicator that the company failed to adapt or even acknowledge its new environment.

In a similar vein, the Wal-Mart habit of encouraging workers to chant "W-A-L-M-A-R-T – *Wal-Mart!*" in a bid to raise morale fitted awkwardly with the German retail culture which often has a works council which deals with group morale. Something akin to a trade union and a "social" team, works councils will often organize staff barbecues, the sports team or the night out, as well as representing workers' concerns at a management level.

Another contributing factor to Wal-Mart's spectacular German failure is the restricted opening hours. While Wal-Mart stores in America are often open "24/7," in Germany this is unheard of, with many shops closed completely on Sunday and other restrictions on opening times.

Finally, the first mistake by Wal-Mart was to appoint a boss for Germany who – incredibly – could not speak German. They followed this by appointing to the top job an Englishman who insisted on running the operation from England.

Rather than being "open in all directions" Wal-Mart was closed in almost all of them. But why should any of these key cultural issues about retail habits have been a surprise to Wal-Mart? They were not state secrets – they were obvious and readily observable facts about the society; yet Wal-Mart was ignorant of them. They had an eye for possibility untutored by an appreciation for diversity or for a cultural perspective other than their own. They were locked into a pattern, apparently incapable of self-reflection and unable to act appropriately. The company was seemingly unable to meet the challenges of a new situation.

Only a company operating with minimal or no levels of diversity and little or no real cultural connections to the country they were operating in, could make so many simple mistakes.

This is a cataclysmic failure of leadership but it is one that we believe could be overcome by long-term commitment to our practices of locating your challenges across the landscapes, acting with equanimity, and aiming for integrated thinking. Engaging diversity is not an abstract notion or a high-minded aspiration; it is an operating principle. In this case, failure to realize this cost one company – the largest employer in the United States – US $1 billion.

4.4.2   KEY PRINCIPLE 2: THE SAFE SPACE TO CREATE

What successful reframing campaigns have in common (e.g. Dove's Campaign for Real Beauty) is that they create a sense of common purpose. For that to prosper, we must have a Safe Space to Create – a shared environment in which diversity can be explored and exchanged and diverse views and visions can coexist, be communicated, and thrive. This fact is *as* important as the existence of constituent elements of diverse viewpoints, attitudes, opinions, reflexes, outlooks, modes, systems, energies, expressions, or skills. Assimilation creates a counterresponse, hostility, and fear. Recognition of difference – unification through separation – leads to common ground. It is only from common ground that we can start moving forward as one.

As a practical tool for decision makers, the lesson is simple. If you want to really harvest the knowledge and wide-ranging views of your staff, they need to be given a platform which is secure and the space to be critical.

At a certain point, diversity for diversity's sake is no good thing. There are limits to what can be a workable team, and efforts to create a "diverse outlook" artificially can result in the "exoticification" of culture or ethnicity or the pigeonholing of people into preconceived stereotypes. Both approaches should be guarded against.

The diverse elements of any project or process need to have some unifying force – otherwise their usefulness degenerates into a cacophony of conflicting views with no common ground. Properly harnessed, a diverse team of thinkers at once practical and grounded and visionary and imaginative, working toward a common goal, can operate as the optimal team. But such a team requires leadership that sees the way opening, that develops and hones a strategy and that offers a context for the team to operate. This is what we call the Safe Space to Create – the shared environment in which diversity can be explored and exchanged so that it can thrive and different voices can be heard, yet that provides the foundations and structures to progress and harness the outcomes of multiple perspectives in a shared and understood way.

With this in place the team's abilities can function and build mutual interdependence; that often means they are able to become considerably more than the sum of their individual parts. The qualities of one outlook bring new dimensions to another; the interchange and synergies bring out previously undisclosed sides into view. This blending and interaction of the team's ability will have the effect of creating a new synthesis, a new higher capacity.

While this is the aim of a team working toward optimal capacity through optimal diversity, there are good reasons why this is resisted. The culture of many companies has been designed to be a closed system aimed at controlling uncertainty, reducing risk, lowering ambiguity, limiting complexity, and ensuring a high level of order and control.

It is therefore the leader's role to open and maintain the Safe Space to Create. Despite these side effects, the rewards of gaining new perspectives are much higher than the risks; new insights stimulate innovation and entrepreneurship, create a competitive edge, and ensure a vibrant and open-minded culture. A high-performing team will also be one that has come to grips with the irreducible differences among team members and will have discovered what is authentically common among them. They will have developed terms of appreciation for one another. So it is not simply an openness to diversity but the integration of diversity in the pursuit of common purpose. Therefore providing a Safe Space to Create is pivotal in bringing about effective diversity and thereby raising the chances for powerful reframing to take place. Such an environment on the team landscape, once established, will be durable, dynamic, and difficult to resist.

Examples of *safe spaces to create* can be very practical, from frequent open, explorative team meetings or off-site retreats to structured technological places where free thought is encouraged and valued. The Internet has over the years produced many ideas and solutions to encourage free thought and powerful exchanges of different perspectives. Traditionally newsgroups and more recently wiki's, blogs, and vlogs are only just a few examples of common spaces where diverse perspectives can get exchanged. Their power is often underestimated in the corporate world, as organizations remain fixed in paradigms of risk and control; yet those organizations that manage to deal with those issues have discovered the tremendous leap forward that can be made by engaging these new approaches and they truly harness diversity of thinking.

One extreme example to contemplate harnessing the power of diversity is the concept of crowdsourcing. In crowdsourcing the job that is traditionally performed by an employee, or team of employees, is now outsourced to an undefined, generally large group of people in the form of an open call over the Internet. Typically the "crowd" consists of amateurs or volunteers, working in their spare time to create content, solve problems or even do some form of R&D.[14] This way, the solutions brought forward are much more tuned to the real needs of its audience, where the crowd even takes control over business processes such as prioritization and scope control.

For instance, Procter & Gamble uses the crowd to solve problems that they cannot solve or address with their internal (9000 people large) corporate R&D division. With the use of a specialized web service (InnoCentive.com) Procter & Gamble taps into the knowledge of a large community of "solvers," offering large cash rewards. "Large" being relative here, as the amount of money offered stands in no comparison to the costs it would otherwise have in trying to solve the problem internally. This is a great example of tapping into a highly diverse crowd, using the Common Space of InnoCentive, to progress on innovation and problem solving.

4.5 Working across the landscapes

As we highlight the power and value of reframing, and have established the conditions for powerful reframing, how does it work across the landscapes? Our discussion so far has, for the sake of illustration, mostly focused on reframing in the context of the organization and team landscape.

Going up to the widest landscapes, we have already described *Blue Ocean* as a landmark for powerfully reframing the industry landscape. Typically in business we put different labels on reframing, such as innovation, creativity, and reinventing – at the heart of each of these terms is the capacity to reframe, as is well illustrated by *Blue Ocean*.

On the macro-business landscape, reframing comes in the form of different perspectives on the context at large, dealing with developments such as socioeconomical changes, technological challenges and disruptions, changing political perspectives, demographic trends, and regulatory changes. As this is the widest perspective, and therefore often the most difficult to comprehend, it is pivotal to have processes in place that guard the organization from frame fixing on this level.

In essence, an organization holds three choices to address this landscape. The first option would be to simply ignore it. As this sounds – and is – a foolish option, it is however what is very often witnessed in practice. Very few strategy processes for instance start from the viewpoint that it is as valuable to gain perspective in what is happening in the world outside the organization and outside its direct zone of influence. The infamous SWOT analysis, in all its variations, quite often implicitly leads the organization to think of its options in terms of its own – frame fixed – sense of reality, thereby ignoring the evolving reality that the organization will live in. Such approaches therefore rather fix the frame, than open it up. In our practices (Chapter 8) we suggest methodologies that do not suffer from this drawback and are therefore highly suitable to include in strategy processes to ensure a wide enough perspective on reality as the organization sets out to determine its position.

A second option would be to create and consider a specific future as a start point and provide this as context in the strategy process. Although this is a step up from not considering any future, it brings a huge risk along, which is focusing on the wrong future. Especially when stakeholders in that future are involved in the future-creation process – which is typically the case as usually the most senior management gets involved in these processes – they have an interest in "believing" a specific future and thereby running a big risk of getting caught in their own fixed paradigms.

The best way to progress reframing on the macro-business landscape, keeping it in line with our arguments on diversity, is therefore to engage in scenario-planning processes, in which multiple futures are explored. Scenario-planning processes and methodologies consider multiple plausible scenarios, usually starting from the most essential uncertainties.

They provide stories and insights into how the landscape might evolve into different, equally plausible directions, and thereby provide a test bed for creating robust and creative strategies, that go beyond gambling for the most desirable future, but take other equally plausible futures into account as well. We illustrate how leaders are adapting through a story about FutureFacts, in Chapter 8.

Going now from the widest landscape, to the nearest, the individual landscape, we arrive at a very challenging level: the leader's own landscape or the landscape level of the self. Here, a different set of questions presents itself. How many things can you do and think? How much diversity can you tolerate? And how much ambiguity and complexity? How do you deal with different perspectives as an individual? Are you ready to move across cultural dimensions? Are you ready (and able) to deal with cultural dilemmas? Are you prepared to bring people into your team who may have a different opinion? How do you hear different opinions? Where do you get the alternative perspective?

All of which are considered in the search for the optimal conditions to stimulate reframing. Yet, surrounding yourself with the best, the most accomplished, and creative mix of people, ideas, or things is rarely the same as maximum diversity. It is often just a cacophony of separate voices. When do you decide that enough is enough?

There is no hard and fast rule for this, but what we want to do is move toward opening assumptive frameworks through constructive dialogue across difference. What do we mean by this? It means being open to change, being able to be flexible enough to alter your own view, to be able to assess and reflect on your core assumptions, and then being able to be fully informed enough to lead. Crucially, it also means to be able to recognize real differences when they exist and not to have them glossed over or absorbed into what one critic of multiculturalism called "a false jubilation." Acknowledging real difference allows people to work together on their common projects, assured that their distinctiveness is recognized and appreciated.

We have asked – through the many questions raised by engaging diversity – when and how do you decide that you have the requisite diversity, that enough is enough? This is what the landscapes offer in our own work: a tool for navigation. We believe that a judgment on requisite diversity will become clear when you have assessed your challenges across the landscapes and composed your response.

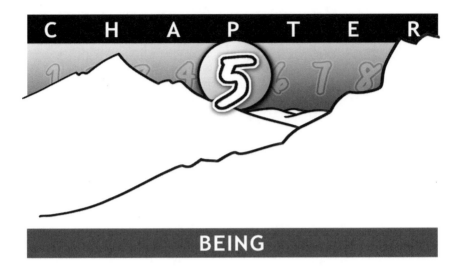

BEING

Leadership Being: Commitment

In Chapter 4, we focused on the *seeing* part of leadership – the ability to see opportunities and reframe realities. It can be associated with the cognitive part of leadership. When we shift our attention to the more emotionally related part of leadership, the *being*, we have found that at the heart of equanimity lies "commitment."

We like to think of commitment as composing the core of who we are, the way in which we express our being in the world over time from the stirring of our early aspirations through the achievements in our productive life to the consolidation of our final legacy. While people tend to hold a host of commitments that weave together as their lives progress, the commitments most pertinent to achieving and sustaining exemplary leadership form a trajectory from aspiration to legacy.

We distinguish three levels of commitment that bond together at any moment in time to provide direction to a leader's action. These are *enduring commitment*, *episodic commitment*, and *immediate intent*. They mostly differ in terms of their scope of time, with *enduring commitments* as the most deeply rooted force, and *immediate intent* as the one we experience most directly. Naturally, they strongly relate, as the deep is often the source for the episodic and the episodic for the immediate.

Before we describe them in more detail, we add that despite the profound impact the dimension of commitment has on one's leadership, we have found that many leaders are not (fully) aware of their own commitments. It is not that they do not have them, but they have often never actively brought them to the surface. In our work with leaders, both in development programs as well as in our coaching, we have found that discovering one's commitments is often one of the most significant and meaningful experiences we can provide to the leaders with whom we work.

5.1 Enduring Commitment

The most sustaining of these commitments that distinguish people who are successful in life and in leadership arise from a deep sense that what we do matters, that there is work to be done, and that we are called to achieve on behalf of some great project, the importance of which goes beyond ourselves. In this perspective, it comes from a spiritually inspired kind of calling, a deeper sense of why it is that we do the things we do.

But it comes not only in response to the call to service. It also springs from the reinforcement of having found for oneself a recurrent sense of a "sweet spot." This is the point at which we come to know from experience, that something we do well and feel fulfilled in doing is a key ingredient that is needed to bring larger "on-behalf-of" ambitions to life and to make larger ambitious enterprises work.

We call this long-term view of what we stand for and work toward, *enduring commitment*.

5.2 Episodic Commitment

We can often trace *enduring commitments* as recurrent threads in one's life tapestry, in terms of how these resurface in ways that are specific to each era or episode of a leader's life. In each episode we see the renewal of *enduring commitment* framed as the foundation and directional energy in addressing central challenges of the life in progress in that particular era. We term this manifestation of *enduring commitment* in a particular phase of a leader's life, *episodic commitment*.

5.3   Immediate Intent

Episodic commitment, the defining quest of each phase is, in turn and in the short run, expressed in what we call, *immediate intent*. Our *immediate intents* drive the actions we are planning or taking in real time on behalf of our commitments.

Commitment is at the heart of the *equanimity shift*. It acts as a directional force in dynamic balance. It relates to equanimity in two ways, which can be thought of as a horizontal and a vertical directional force. First, a leader's *enduring commitments* form the lifeline that runs from the past, orients the present, and projects energy forward toward the immediate task, intermediate projects, the visible horizons of purpose, and then beyond in the direction of what is not yet conceived. In this first way, commitment – enduring, episodic and immediate (intent) – compares to diachronic time, the progressive measure of seconds, minutes, hours, days, months, years, and so forth to eternity. This aspect of commitment works sequentially moving forward by triggering thoughts and initiating actions toward its self-realization. It also works consequentially as we become known for better or for worse for the results of our actions, for what we have or have not accomplished. This diachronic aspect of commitment might be charted or imagined from left to right on a lifeline, hence a horizontal force that supports our movement forward.

Second, commitment forms the platform, the ground, upon which the dynamism of equanimity balances. It anchors the leader's stance, the integration of perspective and purpose that communicates coherence, and authorizes leadership. It stands behind how the leader shows up as present, recovers, and/or reframes in the moment. In this second way, commitment compares to synchronic time; the relational ecology of the whole as it configures in the snapshot of the moment. We see it as a gravitational force, an anchor that provides direction in the moment, for instance when difficult decisions need to be taken.

In Chapter 3, we illustrated *enduring commitment* with the story of Dr Roy Vagelos of Merck[1] who continued to provide support to a long-term drug development, while the odds of commercial success were against it (it is worth reading this story in full if you have not yet, to understand the pressure in this case). One could say that his *enduring commitment* as a scientist and as a human being to create treatments and drugs to help suffering people was his horizontal force that gave him the energy and vision to continue this work. When he changed roles and became the CEO of Merck, with responsibility to look after other interests as well – such as shareholders' interests – the vertical, gravitational force of commitment served him during several *moments of truth* (see Chapter 7), when he had to make difficult decisions that could have easily resulted in ending the program, a decision for which he would probably not even had been blamed by those that had worked on the drug for many years. Yet he did not do so, and continued to respond to his *enduring commitments.*

What sets exemplary leaders apart is that they are sustained in their leadership by their commitments, while on the other side of the coin they sustain and enact their commitments through their leadership. This dynamic of commitments sustaining leaders sustaining commitments unites the diachronic and synchronic aspects of commitment, producing the force field that integrates leadership presence, bringing coherence both to the moment and to the flow of events.

5.4   *Common Fire*

We have already referred several times to the work done in *Common Fire: Leading Lives of Commitment in a Complex World.*[2] Our discussion builds on the legacy of this research, as we have spent the past decade refining and clarifying our own leadership practices. *Common Fire* studied how leaders develop and sustain commitments to work on behalf of a common good larger than themselves. In a process that took more than ten years of interviewing and analysis, nominators identified candidates for interviews who were successful in their particular work, while at the same time bringing awareness of a larger, more complex picture to bear on what they do. We found a certain kind of committed leadership that sees beyond the narrowly partisan and particular to the larger, more complex good of the whole. These leaders construct the good of the enterprises they lead in terms of the larger landscapes that form the wider contexts of their work and their lives.

Like the level 5 leaders in Jim Collins's *Good to Great: Why Some Companies Make the Leap... and Others Don't,*[3] we found a kind of humbleness as we interviewed them, which we linked to the manner in which they worked on behalf of others within and beyond their enterprise. It was seeing themselves as core actors in a complex world, as people who could have a constructive impact at multiple levels as agents of their *enduring commitments* on behalf of the larger goals and enterprise that set them apart. Like the leaders in *Good to Great* they tended to bring out the best in those around them as their sure, consistent sense of meaning and purpose was taken up by colleagues and subordinates alike.

The quality of committed leadership in these exemplars runs deep. It flows through underground streams of *enduring commitment* formed in encounters with diversity, yielding a broader, more inclusive sense of solidarity with people of other opinions, other perspectives and other cultures, whom they would include in the common good toward which they worked.

In *Common Fire* we identified a source of the "on behalf of others" orientation we called, "enlarging encounters across thresholds of difference." Almost as prevalent among the *Common Fire* leaders was the sense of the "sweet spot," a locus in which something deep within the self connects with an area of need in the world. Third was a sense of imagination, which supported what we now call the landscapes and the *eye for possibility.* They could see the big picture, feel at home in the surround, and sense the connections among the points in the web. They knew how to find pathways toward horizons that fortified them and those in their company, moving forward both in the good moments, when losing momentum by admiring accomplishments could set in, and in the tough times, when adversity threatened to sap their strength or worse, immobilize their quest.

In our decade long conversation we have added some new elements to our view of how commitment works in leadership. We can now trace the key role of commitment as the foundation of equanimity in the *Common Fire* leaders, in other exemplars who share their attributes, and for leaders who want to engage and move a complex world. We now understand how the synchronic and diachronic aspects of commitment unite both as foundation and dynamo for equanimity. There is an ancient text that delivers the injunction, "established in being, perform action." Our contemporary reframing goes as follows, "anchored in our being by our enduring commitments, bring these commitments to life by acting from dynamic balance."

5.5 Working with commitment

In our coaching practice, working with commitment is a core element of our approach to help leaders grow. There is not a straightforward structural approach we can provide or a recipe for success in bringing out commitments. But we bring it into the picture through the coaching framework we use in the coaching conversations we maintain.

For this framework, we refer back – and forward – to the *inquiry mapping* process that was briefly described in Chapter 2, and is described in full in Chapter 8. We use an *inquiry map* in our coaching sessions that engages with the following four dimensions:

1. meaning and purpose
2. the project
3. life contours and balances
4. material side.

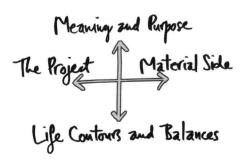

This four dimensional map places *enduring commitment* in the dimension of the meaning and purpose of one's life, of one's highest aspirations, of one's sense of calling, moral compass, and noble causes. The other three dimensions include the episodic and immediate project, life contours and balances and the material side. The episodic and immediate project includes the work one is doing, the leadership context, its goals, strategies, and landscapes of action. Life contours and balances encompass one's present ecology of relationships, interests, avocations, and affiliations as well as one's health and well-being and the intangible assets and challenges therein. The material dimension includes all the objects and financials in one's life, for example, income, house and mortgage, personal property, debts, savings, and so on. We address our four dimensional inquiry map for coaching in Chapter 8.

5.6 Sustaining commitments

As we work with leaders, a key concern is exploring how *immediate intents* line up with the episodic expression of *enduring commitment*.

Enduring commitments may be initiated at any season of one's life. While most of those we found in the *Common Fire* research could be traced to origins in the span of life ranging from childhood to young adulthood, some started later in life. *Enduring commitments* are sustained as recurrent threads in life's tapestry in the form of a defining quest appropriate to that particular episode of one's life and leadership.

That is to say, the same lifeline of *enduring commitment* may emerge through a series of defining quests in the scope of a lifetime.

We use the life of Nelson Mandela as an illustration of commitments – we realize that using Mandela in this context carries the risk of an iconic illustration, as his level of leadership is beyond reach for most of us mortal souls. Yet his life's story does bring out the key points of what commitment means in terms of leadership (in addition, we feel a book on leadership is incomplete if it does not pay tribute in some way to Nelson Mandela, who is in many ways exemplary for contemporary leadership).

At an early age, upon the death of his father, Mandela was taken into the royal residence of the chief, who was acting regent of the Thembu people. There he was raised to become a counselor to the future king, part of the group that would serve as parliament and judiciary in the king's court. In his autobiography, Mandela traces his understanding of leadership[4] to observing the regent and his court.

> The guests would gather in the courtyard in front of the regent's house and he would open the meeting by thanking everyone for coming and explaining why he had summoned them. From that point on he would not utter another word until the meeting was nearing its end. Everyone who wanted to speak did so. It was democracy in its purest form.
>
> The meetings would continue until some kind of consensus was reached. They ended in unanimity or not at all. Democracy meant all men (regardless of status) were to be heard, and a decision taken together as a people. Majority rule was a foreign notion. A minority was not to be crushed by the majority.
>
> As a leader I have always followed the principles I first saw demonstrated by the regent at the great palace.

In this quotation Mandela relates the origin of his enduring commitment to inclusive democracy. This theme shows up recurrently in the seasons of his life, first as the *episodic commitment* of his young adulthood as he dedicated himself to the struggle for equality in South Africa by joining in the non-violent strategies that his people had learned from Gandhi, whose first campaigns were for the rights of immigrants from India living in South Africa.

At 33, three years after the advent of Apartheid, he and his associate, Oliver Tambo, opened the doors of the first black law firm in Johannesburg. During this phase of *episodic commitment* he fortified his quest for inclusive democracy by becoming more deeply involved in the African National Congress (ANC), a multiracial political movement dedicated to reaching the horizon of a democracy in which all South Africans would enjoy equality under the law and the right to vote.

Over the next few years Mandela's *episodic commitment* shifted to fulfilling the requisites of leadership as he and Tambo rose to the helm of the ANC. Then in his 40's, in the wake of the 1959 Sharpsville massacre, when it became clear that the Apartheid government had little hesitation about firing on non-violent protesters, his enduring commitment was reframed as he broke with his personal adherence to non-violent strategies by leading the ANC to adopt a movement to train saboteurs for action against Apartheid's military and government targets. Still, in this new *episodic commitment* he maintained his long-term concern for the eventual healing of South African society by always taking care for "life and limb." For this initiative, he became an outlaw and eventually was captured and convicted in 1964 of several crimes against the state.

Now in midlife, Mandela faced the likelihood of a sentence either of death or life imprisonment. His *enduring commitment* now expressed itself in the immediate intent of using the public forum afforded him by his trial to advance his core cause. At his trial, Mandela explained his intention:

> We in the ANC have always stood for non-racial democracy, and we shrank from any action which might drive the races further apart than they already were. But the hard facts were that fifty years of non-violence had brought the African people nothing but more repressive legislation, and fewer and fewer rights. It may not be easy for this court to understand, but it is a fact that for a long time the people had been talking of violence – of the day when they would fight the white man and win back their country, and we the leaders of the ANC, had nevertheless always prevailed upon them to avoid violence and use peaceful methods. While some of us discussed this in May and June of 1961, it could not be denied that our policy to achieve a non-racial state by non-violence had achieved nothing, and that our followers were beginning to lose confidence in this policy and were developing disturbing ideas of terrorism...When we took [the decision to conduct a campaign of sabotage] the ANC heritage of non-violence and racial harmony was very much with us. We felt the country was drifting towards a civil war in which blacks and whites would fight each other. We viewed the situation with alarm. Civil war would mean the destruction of what the ANC [and what Mandela's *enduring commitment*) stood for: with civil war racial peace would be more difficult than ever to achieve.[5]

Mandela concluded his *episodic commitment* as active leader of the sword of the nation by exercising his immediate intent to project his cause and presence with concluding words that echoed in the silence of his imprisonment for more than two decades to come.

> During my lifetime I have dedicated myself to this struggle of the African people. I have fought against white domination, and I have fought against black domination. I have cherished the ideal of a democratic and free society in which all persons live together in harmony and with equal opportunities. It is an ideal which I hope to live for and achieve. But if needs be it is an ideal for which I am prepared to die.[6]

During his long imprisonment, his *episodic commitment* turned toward the hope that he would someday be released and toward the secret preparation of his biography as a legacy in the event of either his release or death in prison. Then came the thaw during which a new Minister of Justice of the Apartheid government, working in collaboration with the core set of Ministers who would eventually bring an end to Apartheid, began to reintroduce him surreptitiously to the world from which he had been secluded for a quarter of a century. At this time his *episodic commitment* came to preparing himself to prevail in his negotiations on behalf of the realization of his *enduring commitment*, through a series of immediate commitments that are well captured in subsequent biographies.

That Mandela had always opposed targeting civilians with a campaign of terror made it possible for him to conclude this phase of *episodic commitment* through the immediate intent of the negotiations themselves which established a new future for South Africa. President F.W. deKlerk, the new leader of the Apartheid government, who had taken the bold and constructive action of ending that policy and releasing him from prison, became both partner and adversary in those talks for which the two leaders were named Nobel Peace Laureates. In this context, Mandela essentially traded the threat of violence for a collaborative approach to building a South Africa in which all adult citizens would cast votes of equal weight regardless of their color or status, thus bringing to realization his most *enduring commitment*.

But the narrative of commitment continued, as Mandela's new episodic intent on behalf of his *enduring commitment* was the initiation of inclusive democracy itself through his campaign to become the first black president of a multiracial South Africa. In 1994, now past his seventy-fifth birthday, he won the election and established a multiracial unity government that included deKlerk, whom he had defeated at the polls.

As president his *episodic commitment* became establishing an honestly functioning representative government while working toward reconciliation of his nation's ethnic groups. Harkening back to the regent's courtyard of his childhood, where everyone who wanted to speak had a chance to do so, he established The Truth and Reconciliation Commission, in which the brutal transgressions of the shrouded past could be revealed by admissions of guilt in return for amnesty. Fellow Nobel Peace Laureate, Archbishop Desmond Tutu, who had become South Africa's chief voice for non-violence in the decade before Mandela's release, now presided much in the manner of the regent, as he led South Africa in weeping as atrocities were recounted. Through the work of this commission, the two leaders sought to establish a common, public account of the past as a legacy to buttress the future of inclusive democracy.

In what may be considered a crowning fulfillment of his *enduring commitment*, Mandela concluded his formal leadership by enacting perhaps the greatest legacy that he, as the first fully elected democratic leader of his country, could leave to his fellow citizens – to step down from the presidency at the end of his elected term.

In this brief review of Mandela's life we see the origin of an *enduring commitment* as well as how it was expressed in the quests associated with major life episodes. Instances of leadership on behalf of each episodic quest embodied *enduring commitment* in the manner in which we usually see it enacted. That is, as the *immediate intent* of each synchronic moment moving in the diachronic flow of the leader's trajectory. Or, stated more simply, we see the leader centered in dynamic balance by *enduring commitment*, acting in the flow of leadership.

CHAPTER 6

DOING

Leadership Doing: How We Recover and Radiate Presence

We described equanimity as the ability to maintain dynamic balance and overcome disorientation in a fast-changing, information-rich environment. Perhaps when we use these words, people imagine dynamic balance to be something akin to Buddhist meditation or the latest health craze. While these may be worthy pursuits, the leaders we work with live in a world where fast action and difficult decisions are required. Yet even in the extreme pace set by competitors and market conditions, we have come across leaders who were "graceful while in motion," fully present to everyone they met, and artful in their ability to recover from most situations they faced in their work and their lives. To highlight these qualities, let us jumpstart with a noisy evening in the Boston Garden, a center for basketball lovers around the world, then go to a counterexample with Salomon Brothers, and conclude with a remarkable Chilean business leader.

The scene is the fifth game of the 1987 NBA Eastern Final Series in basketball between the Boston Celtics and the Detroit Pistons. The winner of this best of seven series will go on to face the L.A. Lakers in the Championship series.

The defending champion Celtics are hurting, led by the legendary Larry Bird, the league's most valuable player for the past three seasons. They have lost super-subs Bill Walton and Scott Wedman to injuries and future NBA Hall of Famer Kevin McHale, though playing, is limping badly. The situation is dire for the Celtics. The game clock is down to the final two seconds.

The Celtics, behind by one point to the Pistons, have just lost the ball out of bounds on what looks like their final possession. They are about to go down three games to two with the series riding on the next game where the Pistons will enjoy the advantage of home court. Detroit's big man, Bill Lambeer, stands close to the basket where he and his team mates just two seconds earlier successfully defended against the Celtics' final desperate attempt to score. Future Hall of Famer, Isiah Thomas, inbounds the ball to Lambeer from the sideline as the other players head toward the far end of the court.

Suddenly everything changes as Larry Bird, the Celtics' leader on the court, shifts direction from heading down court and lunges for the pass from Thomas to Lambeer. Bird gets his hand on the ball and in the same motion flips a perfect pass to teammate Dennis Johnson who has reversed his motion in perfect synchrony with Bird's and is headed back toward the basket. The pass reaches Johnson in perfect stride and he lays the basketball up and into the basket as the final second ticks off the clock.

With this stunning reversal of fortune, Larry Bird snatches victory from the jaws of defeat and leads Dennis Johnson and his other teammates into the NBA finals.

When Larry Bird was growing up, he attracted enough attention beyond the hamlet of French Lick to be recruited by coach Bobby Knight to play at the University of Indiana. People knew he was tall and had a lot of talent, but he also clearly lacked a couple of key ingredients to be a top level player. He was at least a step too slow to play away from the basket and he did not jump high enough to make him a great talent closer to the basket. After an alienating few months at the University of Indiana, Larry Bird was back in French Lick collecting other people's garbage and, of course, spending his spare time working at the game he loved. The next four years found him enrolled again in college, this time at Indiana State, a basketball backwater compared to coach Knight's powerhouse across the state. Over the next couple of years the man who some came to call Larry Legend, began to emerge.

Still lacking swiftness of foot and much in the way of jumping ability, Larry Bird became one of the handful of greatest players in the history of the game because of his leadership presence on the court. He was one of those rare great players who not only excelled in his own feats but also made the players around him better individually and as a team. How did he do it? Larry Bird played, for the most part, with equanimity: dynamic balance that held the focus of immediate intent of each play rooted in a deep commitment to winning, his mental/emotional state was pure willingness on the court. He would dive for the loose balls and mix it up underneath getting himself in the best rebounding position and holding it tenaciously, playing with the zest of an artist actualizing the flow of performance, exerting a presence on the court that affected the play of teammates and opposition players alike.

He had an acute *eye for possibility*. Not only could he use his outstanding peripheral vision to see the court in more dimensions than most other players, he also grasped the developmental trajectory of each of those dimensions in the same moment of vision. This permitted him to anticipate what was about to happen and to reframe his approach in the flow of the action so as to be in a position to affect the next event. Bird, playing in dynamic balance, saw a new possibility: Lambeer was standing too flat-footed, not on his toes breaking toward the ball, leaving an inadvertent opening. Recovering from the momentum of the previous play with its unmistakable foreboding of loss, by inserting himself willingly and in flow, Bird reframed the situation, not only for himself but for his teammate who scored the winning basket.

You might think while reading this story that this was just a lucky steal, just a moment of luck blown out of proportion because of the dramatic consequences. But we challenge you to review your question at the end of this chapter, as we have learned to understand what leadership doing entails. The effect of presence is often most visible in sports teams, because it has a direct impact on the immediate, tangible outcome, the result of the game. It shows its impact, an impact that goes beyond the technical qualities and skills of the individual. Their mere presence adds power to the team, and makes the team perform better.

After having explored *seeing* and *being* in the previous two chapters, we arrive at the third leg of our leadership triangle: *doing*. Having all the equanimity attributes work for him in this heroic moment would have gone unnoticed if Larry Bird had not translated it into the one thing that physically created the steal: having the presence to make the right decision at the right time. Let us not underestimate how much decision making and acting are a key part of leadership. Where Chapters 4 and 5 focused foremost on the internals of leadership, we now focus attention on the "*doing*" aspect of leadership. *Doing* is about how leadership plays out in real life. It is in a way the external face of leadership. Making decisions is a pivotal activity in that respect and relates directly the two attributes we develop further in the following pages, *projecting presence* and *recovering oneself.*

6.1   Action and decision taking

We have charged our leaders with big responsibilities, and with such responsibilities goes the obligation to take decisions. Rattan Chada, the founder of Mexx – a large fashion retail chain – recently told us: "There is only one thing that CEOs must do. And that is: do their job." It is the single observation that the lead role carries with it – the obligation to make the decisions when needed. People that move up the ladder in organizations are repeatedly told to delegate more and more. This gives way to the idea that delegation is all that matters at the top of the house. This is a false idea. We do expect leaders to make the tough decisions. Surely, this must be well thought through, in concert with the team and all the other things we know about winning decisions, but decisions are what leaders must make.

Now, there is much to be said about that "simple" observation: leadership is also about taking decisions. Of course it is, but that does not mean that this is a straightforward process. Decision taking is inherently a risky process and requires courage and guts at given moments. As with decision making there are significant risks involved – risks in making the wrong decisions, as well as risks by not taking decisions (as we will see in the case of Salomon Inc. that follows). So, it is not just about making decisions, but *making the right decisions at the right time.*

How do the masters of decision making do it? By seeking to stay in balance, in even the most pressurized, stressful situations, and by taking the really big decisions with a practiced consciousness of the wider landscape shaping that decision.

Conscious decision making *and* being aware of the wider landscape suggests that leaders raise their game to a new level. It requires that we consider: How do we know when we are making fully conscious decisions? And how should we think about timing? If we do not make a decision immediately, what is the difference between procrastinating and paralysis and purposeful temporizing? If we consider decision making as one form of action required of leaders, we can explore both questions through the two remaining *equanimity shift* attributes: *being present* and *projecting presence*, and *recovering oneself* before getting close to the paralysis zone. We advocate that both are directly related to the core leadership activity, *doing*, which includes deciding and acting.

6.2 Making conscious decisions (or not), and the risk of slipping into irrecoverable territory

We will borrow a second example from Michael Useem's thinking about the *Leadership Moment*,[1] the case in which he describes the downfall of Salomon Inc. and its subsidiary Salomon Brothers. In the late 1980s and early 1990s, Salomon was one of the formidable Wall Street brokers. It claimed additional fame as it featured in Michael Lewis' Liar's Poker, a classic tale of Wall Street macho-ism. The firm was headed by John H. Gutfreund, who had featured in *Business Week* as the "King of Wall Street." Salomon was a real player on Wall Street, one that had great respect among its peers. Hosting a strong, aggressive, capitalistic company culture, it seemed to have the right spirit to combat in the Wall Street jungle.

One of its cornerstone businesses was U.S. debt trading. The team of bond traders, headed by the legendary John Meriwether who was featured in Liars Poker, was extremely successful and valuable to the firm. In 1990, they were responsible for US $400 million in company earnings. Having a privileged position as one of the 39 primary dealers that are allowed to bid for newly issued government bonds, Salomon had access to a vast market and was amongst those 39 primary dealers, one of the biggest and most powerful players.

With the privilege of being a primary dealer came some obligations and restrictions as well. The government, who clearly benefited from a well-functioning market for its newly issued bonds, was not served by one or more overly powerful firms, and had therefore restricted the sales to one individual firm in a new auction to not go over a maximum of 35 percent of the total volume available. However, that was the maximum the firm could buy for its own books. In addition to that, it could place bids from its clients, such as the big pension funds, the World Bank and other major players that wanted to secure their funds in government bonds.

On April 27, 1991, one of the top traders, Paul Mozer, walked into the office of his boss, John Meriwether, to confess his wrongdoing in an auction held on February 21. In order to access more than the restricted 35 percent of the market, he had placed an additional bid in the name of one of his clients, S.G. Warburg. However, he had used Warburg's name to simulate a client, in order to acquire more than its maximum 35 percent slot. Picking Warburg as a bogus client had been a bad choice, as, unknown to Mozer, Warburg had itself also bid for the auction, being a primary dealer itself. This alarmed the treasury officials, who started an investigation. Despite his attempts to cover up, Mozer soon realized that he was not going to be able to hide his action much longer and confessed to his boss.

Meriwether informed the president and legal council, and reached John Gutfreund, the CEO, in the evening. The next day, they discussed the matter internally. This was against the context that Paul Mozer had been in trouble before and was not at all in friendly waters with the government officials. Given Mozer's formal position as "managing director," only John Gutfreund could take disciplinary action against him. But he did not. Nor did he take action to inform the treasury officials of the news that had reached him. He was simply hoping the issue would go away.

Not having felt any consequences, Paul Mozer submitted another illegal bid on May 22, this time using Tiger Investments and Quantum Fund as bogus client orders. The bid, which went together with Salomon's own bid, was so sharply priced by Mozer, that he virtually won the entire bid (86 percent). This resulted in a strategic position for Salomon, who now dominated the market, as other primary players had to borrow from Salomon to live up to their own customer obligations. The virtual monopoly that Salomon had created in the May 22 bid did not go unnoticed, as other players complained, and the Securities and Exchange Commission (SEC) and the Treasury started a secret investigation into this auction.

Despite the damage that was building up, John Gutfreund had until mid-summer 1991 still not decided on disciplinary actions against Mozer, nor had he informed the officials. An internal investigation at Salomon showed that the issue was even worse, as similar misbehavior had appeared in a December 1990 auction, as well as in the February 11 and in April auctions. Altogether this had amounted to a major compliance issue that became impossible to ignore.

Finally, on August 8, more than three months after having first heard of the illegalities, Gutfreund took action and called the officials at the Federal Reserve, the Treasury, and the SEC. The following day Salomon issued a press release about the wrongdoing and soon after made it public that the CEO had known of the violations since April. From there on it pretty much spun out of control for Gutfreund. Holders of Salomon's own debt requested their money back, and as this floodgate opened, Salomon was forced in the afternoon to suspend trading in its own securities. Officials informed Gutfreund in the evening that they were considering ending Salomon's primary dealer status. The next day, John Gutfreund, who had been with the firm since 1953, resigned.

In this classic case of damage through non-action, what stands out is that during the unfolding events nobody took a moment to seriously reflect on what was at hand here. The top management's original judgment call on

April 29, when the news was first brought to their attention, that Mozer's action was improper but not unlawful, had alienated them from the context in which this played. Viewed as an issue on the Organization Landscape – an internal matter where an employee portrayed undesired behavior – they failed to see the wider context of this issue. If they had bumped up the issue to the *industry and markets landscape*, they would have realized that such behavior in the context of alarmed officials, inappropriately treated colleague dealers, abused clients, and damaging investor relationships, would require much firmer attention. Also, John Gutfreund had a dominant position on Wall Street and its global network of people and institutions. This required him to be all over the globe. His travel schemes in that period were horrendous, flying all across the planet to attend meetings and functions, he hardly had time for what Rattan Chada called: "Just do your job." Gutfreund's successor, Deryck Maughan, appointed by Warren Buffet who stepped in as crisis manager immediately following Gutfreund's resignation, reflected later: "In a very complex, very large, diversified institution, somebody has to be looking after the shop, asking the questions, and providing direction and leadership."

As we will see in Chapter 7, there is an art to recognizing the *moments of truth*, the moments where leadership is called for and where action is not just appropriate but required. Gutfreund did not just lose his job over this episode but was fined US $100,000 and was banned for life from serving as a chairman or CEO of a securities firm. Paul Mozer was jailed for four months, fined US $1.1 million, and banned from the securities industry for life. The company stock went into a freefall, loosing US $1.65 billion in just one day and the company had to pay out damage settlements amounting up to US $290 million in the months to follow.

Gutfreund's behavior clearly illustrates the need for making the right decisions at the right time. It is a case in which the lack of conscious and purposeful action caused greater damage than immediate action might have done. Not only would Mozer no longer have had a chance to continue his practice, the reputational damage would have been far less, as Salomon could have demonstrated that while it played hard ball it also had zero tolerance for not abiding by the rules.

Many writers have tackled the question of management decision making, for example Graham Alison's work on the Cuban missile crisis described in the *Essence of Decision: Explaining the Cuban Missile Crisis.*[2] Or J Harvey's hilarious description of the *Abilene Paradox*[3] or Fons Trompenaars' essay on *Did the Pedestrian Die?: Insights from the World's Greatest Culture Guru.*[4] These all point to the challenges of working through dilemmas and making decisions and where decision making goes wrong. Yet our concern for the time being is about how leaders cultivate and sustain a presence of mind and recover from the "deer in the headlights" syndrome quickly enough during those moments of decision, these Moments Of Truth (see Chapter 7). Once again, it is not that great leaders do not know how to make decisions or act. What keeps them from making use of all the good advice and empirical research available is that when caught in the clutches of a decision, they have not practiced two essential elements of equanimity across the landscapes of their leadership: being present and *projecting presence* and rapid recovery.

This story highlights the question, how does decision making relate to our two remaining equanimity attributes of *presence* and *recovery*? Let us continue to discover.

6.3　Being Present and Projecting Presence

In heroic sports moments, such as Larry Bird's steal in our example that heads this chapter, dynamic balance and presence are happening simultaneously. We can see how Larry Bird exerted his presence to clinch victory and we can imagine the bodily dynamic balance he displayed in the economy of making two plays with a single motion. In our view of equanimity, though, exercising presence is not usually all that dramatic, but the dynamic balance is usually there beneath the surface. His single-motion steal and assist on Dennis Johnson's winning basket is as clear a demonstration of court presence ever witnessed.

Presence is about how leaders show up on the stage of action. *Presence*, as we see it, builds up through your track record of *doing*. This includes your decision making; when done with integrity and authenticity, it all adds up to your *presence* as a leader, and yet the idea of *presence* takes some further explanation.

Start by considering: we know when someone is with us, but not present. There is even a new word for it: presenteeism. In contrast to absenteeism, one is physically present but mentally and emotionally absent. So exercising presence is an active state. This takes us to two forms of *presence* that we find helpful for leaders to cultivate: being present where you are and being conscious of your *presence*.

6.3.1　PRESENCE IN RELATIONSHIP TO LEADERSHIP LANDSCAPES

Focus if you will, on the organizational landscape – leaders must do more than face tough decisions about their enterprise. They must also project their *presence*, their influence throughout the enterprise by being alert and responsive to the organization's story – its history, its values, its vision, its people. It is the leader's role to tell that story so that it is heard throughout the organization and to live the story in ways that are authentic.

The story needs to be both visionary and real, connecting past legacies to the current situation and the present to a compelling vision at the horizon, while also addressing key questions. How does the organization function? Is it fit for its purpose? Where is it now and where is it going? What is the best direction to get there? What needs to be maintained and what might need to change for the organization to fulfill its highest purposes?

Beyond these general questions there are the specific questions of *projecting presence*. What is happening now? How is the story best retold now given the immediate challenges and the shifting circumstances that everyone is aware of? How does the leader incorporate emerging challenges into the story?

Leadership *presence* works a bit differently when the leader switches from a primary focus on the organization landscape to the leadership team. *Being present* and *projecting presence* in an organization setting does not always require physical presence. People often experience the "signature" of a leader in the form of repeated messages, generous acts, or leitmotivs that each in their own way express a higher than average level of consciousness about the needs of the organization. In contrast, presencing work with one's team is a face-to-face, day-to-day challenge that raises a number of questions: How does a leader remain fully present in a conversation with each individual team member and with the whole team? How does the leader open space for conversation and develop a culture of authentic listening? Our colleague and noted psychiatrist Theo Compernolle is a leading thinker on the topic of stress. He notices how people experience negative stress when people do not listen. "When I ask children to draw pictures of adults, they draw a big round face, with big eyes and a big smiling face. Then they draw very tiny ears – and sometimes there are no ears on their drawings!"

In a series of workshops with the industrial group Philips, we ask leaders to practice their *presence* by noticing the style of their colleagues and noticing their own signature. We draw on the work of a noted choreographer Laban to make the point (Laban Movement Analysis, was created by Rudolf Laban (*c.* 1879–1958), a pioneer in movement research. As Laban was developing a way to write about human movement, he uncovered basic principles of form, sequence, and dynamics). Each delegate is asked to consider whether their contact with others is "light or heavy, fast or slow, direct or indirect" and then act out the different styles. While the experience of being something other than your natural style leads to hilarious and uncomfortable interactions, the simple point is clear: our *presence* as leaders is experienced through others, and those moments with one another offer the possibility to choose between conscious powerful *presence* or distracted, detached presenteeism.

One of the more subtle dangers a leader can face is a short circuit in feedback coming up through the organization. Leaders need to know not only how each team member is doing on assignments and deliverables, but also what stands out for each team member, what challenges, concerns, surprises, puzzles, or frustrates them, and what opportunities are emerging. SHV, a very successful 300-year-old family business we work with, has a set of core values crafted by a master of presence whose signature is still felt after his untimely passage. Paul Fentener van Vlissingen's character and physical *presence* echo around the world in a simple set of values he created through discussions with his leaders. One of the most memorable and surprising of these was "Bad News Must Travel Fast. Good News Can Take Its Time." This was Paul's explicit effort to ensure that feedback was always welcome, especially errors that could be corrected in a timely manner. So *presence* is not always good news, and its effects can be felt in the walls for years.

By creating an atmosphere of mutuality with each team member, the leader is in the best position to articulate goals and expectations, while coaching the team member toward optimal performance in ways that the team member can hear, accept, and make use of. Moreover, the leader presencing through mutuality, usually gets a much better read on the organizational territory of each team member and is in the optimal position to hear useful feedback from each perspective.

Practicing *presence* with an intention to build trust and mutuality with each team member enhances a leader's *presence* with the leadership team as a whole. The leader who exercises *presence*, starts by being alert to the dynamics of the team, driving toward optimal performance and synergies while leading the team in creating, living, and telling the stories of its members' mutual journey. While working with the new Executive Committee team of the Belgian Post on their vision, we worked with them to create an unconventional path toward a vision. Instead of starting the vision conversation on the wider landscapes of stakeholder, Industry and Organization, their energetic leader Johnny Thijs began by asking everyone on the team to describe what brought this rich mix of leaders and talents – with experience in consulting, logistics, brewing, and finance - to the Belgian Post. A few common threads emerged from the diverse team: to serve their communities, to make a difference, to change the industry, and to shift the performance assumptions of the company. A vision of the Post quickly followed from the mutual trust and appreciation that grew out of that first conversation. It simply demanded that the leader be conscious of his *presence* and lead by example.

The above story suggests that *presence* is also a matter of setting the standard of performance for the team through self-conduct – the area over which the leader, in the end, has the greatest control. Self-conduct emanates from the personal landscape of the leader. The presencing function of the landscape master tool supports the leader in a stance of dynamic balance wherever they show up.

At the landscape of the individual leader, this means that performance on the immediate set of projects is likely to be optimal if the leadership work reflects the leader's abiding commitments. Those leaders who can express their deep intentions and thrive in the story line of their life's contours and balances will convey it to those in their presence. It is equally important that there are material means to support the projects – money to drive the project or resources to support it – and that the leader feels well rewarded for the work. Deficits in any of these areas can undermine the leader's capacity to sustain dynamic balance and be fully present.

Likewise, when moving to the landscape of the market or industry, the leader has to be able to appraise the competitiveness of the organization with an eye to both long- and short-term performance, to movements in their markets, and to growth potential. In this case, the presencing function is more akin to a view from a helicopter, taking the leader to a panoramic view of the emerging conditions, innovations, and shifts that are effecting or could soon affect the organization's performance.

Presence expressed from an overview of the landscape also pertains to other wider contexts in which an organization operates, particularly the political, social, technological, and environmental changes that society and the world are experiencing. Finally, the helicopter vision can be used to survey the economic climate of the surround as it affects the market within which the enterprise competes.

6.4 Recovery

If *presence* is about how leaders show up in action, then *recovery* is how leaders deal with unexpected situations and challenges that complicate their ability to act. As the late John Lennon famously put it: "Life is what happens to you while you are busy making other plans." It is indeed that we can see, anticipate, and plan our actions, but reality is that we live in a world in which we regularly are pushed offbalance. Consequently, in our leadership roles, we must master our ability to recover, to bring us back to equanimity. The other qualities of equanimity – reframing, an *eye for possibility*, sustaining *presence*, and holding to our commitments – in some ways depend on the capacity to recover oneself. For without *recovery* the mental, physical, emotional, and spiritual aspects of leadership become a drain rather than a wellspring of energy and vitality. A closer examination of *recovery* will take us to an understanding that when difficult and surprising moments arise (sometimes more than once a day), we can bounce back quickly before we lose the confidence of those we lead.

A fascinating aspect of *recovery* has emerged from our research and practice: those leaders who seem to be masters of *recovery* rarely see it as anything remarkable or special. They have a built-in equanimity that views most events in life as threads to be woven into the fabric of their story, so their capacity to recover seems to come from an almost natural resilience to life's and work's challenges. For the rest of us mortals, it is practice, practice, and practice.

6.4.1 THE REMARKABLE DR JUAN RADA

Nearly twenty years ago, our paths crossed with a brilliant young academic from Chile named Dr Juan Rada. At the time, he had recently moved from Paris to Geneva to take up a post as a research fellow at the International Management Institute, the predecessor of the IMD, then led by Dr Bodan Hawrylyshyn. Dr Rada had recently been identified as a rising star in the management of innovation field, for his early understanding of how transborder data flows in the automobile industry would herald a new world of cross-border networks and a new service economy where value could be created and transferred from place to place, anywhere in the world.

Within months he had become the youngest member of the Club of Rome and was courted by leaders from across Europe for his advice on the future of technology and services. Within two years at the Institute, he was appointed Director General and led in the creation of IMD, now ranked among the finest Business Schools in the world. From a distance it appeared as if he progressed from success to success in an inexorable rise to the top. But Dr. Rada had seen darker days. As a student in the Catholic University of Santiago, he had lived through the events that transpired in 1973 when Augusto Pinochet participated in a *coup d'état* that established a military government and deposed the democratically elected President Salvador Allende. Were it not for a fortuitous turn of events – a scholarship, a friendly embassy, and an airplane in the night – Juan might have suffered the same fate as 3000 other declared "leftists" including his closest friends, who were herded into the national stadium and summarily shot. If he had been slightly unluckier, he might have been one of the 30,000 who went missing during Pinochet's rule. Fortunately his life had bigger plans for him. Thanks to some scholarship money and an advanced degree, he found his way abroad. Under a spotlight, his story is one of long years of uncertainty and sadness about the fate of his family and friends and the demands of learning in first English then in French to complete a doctorate. Ultimately, he had to overcome the tension in his life that arose from his existential situation – join the activists who longed for the return of democratic rule in Chile or start a new life. He describes his tragedy and recovery in this way:

> One day you are happy, living with your family and friends and going to University. Within a few short years, you are standing on a street in Paris. Your hopes, your role in life, your history is completely interrupted and destroyed. It happens brutally. You go to sleep, wake up and it's not there any more.

He continued:

> This was a harsh experience. Reflect, re-think and then rebuild from scratch. I kept reminding myself of a saying: you cannot cry for the dead, you have to build the future forward and turn the page. This does not mean ignore the emotions of the time. The emotional experience was so strong – too strong. I have fresher memories of that period than any other time in my life. At the same time, I began to re-think everything. My entire youth was consumed with the distribution of income. I later reflected that I had no idea how wealth was created. Was I really understanding how an economy works? I spent many months in the Venezuelan Embassy, then went to Paris with $200 in my pocket. You always feel guilty for not going back. Yet I made a set of decisions that made me not fit for going back. I kept reminding myself of one determining factor: my life was not finished. Friends had perished. Then you question yourself to the bone. No stone remained unturned. You still have to build a horizon.

Once Juan was underway with his life's recovery, there remained an *eye for possibility*. He continued:

> I could not go back. I took the conscious decision to live my life here in Europe as I see fit – not as an exile in an exiled community. I remember

arriving in Paris and staring at the Paris phone books in the phone booth – 5 or 6 books just for Paris, and I did not know anyone. Yet I had to go on with my life. It was a liberating feeling. I was free from the social and political constraints of my home country. Being free from social constraints is one of the features of increasing globalisation. Would Ghoshan of Nissan/Renault – a Brazilian – be as successful in Brazil?

We spoke of enduring commitments in the mosaic of his life:

I have an enduring commitment to human rights. When you experienced a lack of human rights in Chile, it gives you a sense of how justice can be different. You have no idea how important human rights are, until you see them disappear. My company now works in Bosnia to re-construct the registers. Ethnic cleansing is the idea that you no longer exist. You go to the bank and no one will validate who you are. This is hard to imagine in any country that claims to be civilized, let alone one that is within a one hour flight from here.

And so Rada continues his human rights work and adds this to his work with the International Union for the Conservation of Nature and his occasional collaboration with the International Labor Office. Lastly, an important part of Juan's story was maintaining a sense of hope:

I never imagined hopelessness. I never believed I was a victim. If I had chosen to be part of the exile community, I would be a victim. My self affirmation was: dry your tears. Look forward not backward. Many successful people have turned the page. Faced the facts. Reconciling the reality of the situation, perhaps in some parts of the world, social peace is more important than justice. To achieve justice you would have to give up the pure notion of social peace. For me, to build the future, you need peace more than justice. The liberating thought is that there is always life after horrible experiences. Your life is not extinguished by the destruction of your circumstances.

Today Juan has global responsibility for Public Institutional Clients on the managing board of Oracle. He has a passion for early maps of the Americas and has hopes of establishing a forest reserve to research environmental sustainability in southern Chile. Recovery.

In radically new situations, ones that push us offbalance, having a set of recovery mechanisms at hand becomes vital. A leader's life is fortunately not always as dramatic as Juan Rada's. Yet dealing with unforeseen situations happens in every leader's life, and it is often at those moments that leadership is called for. As a leader, one must therefore master the art of *recovery*, to ensure you do not overshoot, nor undershoot, the situation. Only when one succeeds in bouncing back to equanimity, will they be able to deal with the situation in a masterful way. The pieces of the equanimity puzzle fit together: regain an ability to reframe, seek out new possibilities, and radiate *presence* even in the most desperate of times.

Our earlier example of Salomon illustrates how great leaders deal with such situations. Sadly not John Gutfreund, as he had moved out of vision. But Warren Buffett, who stepped in as interim chairman and CEO manager the very moment Gutfreund stepped down. Buffett, who was the largest Salomon stockholder (and today one of the world's richest people according to Forbes), took on the role of interim chairman and CEO. His first challenge came minutes before he was appointed, when he learned that government officials would announce that Salomon would be suspended from bidding on the next Treasury auction. Buffett recognized this news immediately as a *moment of truth*, as it would have a devastating effect on Salomon, given its financial implications. Being already severely damaged by its management crisis, its loss of faith, and its very uncertain future ahead, adding further and immediate financial damage to its problems would probably take away any chance for recovery. He therefore immediately called the officials and – after hours of frantic calls – convinced them to halt their decision, at least temporarily, so the organization could recollect itself in the face of this rapidly unfolding news.

In the short period that followed, Buffett took firm action. He understood the consequences of the situation Salomon had been brought into and recognized that the only way out was through restoring its credibility. His first actions were oriented toward mending the organization, that was called "rotten to the bone" by some officials. He assigned himself the role of Chief Compliance Officer and announced a shockingly strict set of rules. He did the same externally. He communicated full cooperation with the federal regulators and investigators and actively ensured the cooperation. The day after he was appointed interim chairman, he visited the chairman of the SEC, Richard Breeden. Expecting Buffett would need a lesson in compliance, and a severe warning to cooperate, he told Buffett that he would turn over every stone and would not rest until all obstructions had been uncovered and dealt with. Buffett, who did not need to be convinced of that, responded "Call us anytime someone doesn't give you what you want, you will have a new person to deal with in twenty minutes."

Eventually, the government did not bring criminal indictments to Salomon, largely as a result of Buffett's immediate and decisive actions to restore credibility and to fully comply and cooperate with the officials as well as a result of Buffett's impeccable reputation.

As we reflect on how Buffett recovered the situation, which was daunting and critical in the early days of his appointment as interim CEO and chairman, we can establish that this was a man who acted from a position of full dynamic balance. The stakes were high for Buffett as well – as the company's largest stockholder, he had US $700 million at stake. Yet, despite this potential loss, he acted in balance, and set the company on a course of a radically different corporate culture. Working at Salomon Brothers was not your average job – the free-riders trader mentality was rooted deeply in every individual and in its culture, so migrating to a culture of compliance was bound to meet tough resistance.

Yet to Buffett this was the only way out. Having carefully gained and maintained his impeccable status, he had an immediate intent not to be associated with any further wrongdoing. And his *presence* as a leader played an important role in the government's decision not to press criminal charges.

As a final aside to this story, and to relate back to our *equanimity shift* and regaining dynamic balance, Buffett clearly portrays these qualities in a speech he gave on August 26, 1991. Just to recall, this was barely one week after the news had broken and forced Gutfreund to resign. One can only imagine the despair the company was faced with at that moment in time. Buffett spoke on that occasion to all gathered Salomon employees, and started to press the importance of now "doing first-class business in a first-class way." As he continued to speak, he directed his audience as follows:

> Also, I expect you to get out and do a lot of business. The "first-class business in a first-class way" does not preclude in any way doing a lot of business; it doesn't preclude gutsy business. It just means you keep the ball rolling in the middle of the court … If you lose money for the firm by bad decisions, like I've done plenty of times for Berkshire, I will be very understanding. If you lose reputation for the firm, I will be ruthless … What kind of a firm can come out of this? Well, in that regard I may have a loftier vision than virtually anyone, because I think great things can come out of this … We have a chance to preserve all of the strengths of the past and have people look at us with a new eye … I think in the end we'll be more proud of this company than you've ever been before.

Recovery and *presence* are two of the five leadership qualities of equanimity. While these stories are drawn from a range of remarkable experiences, there is a common thread: each protagonist showed a capacity or lack of capacity to use these qualities. As we shall see later in this book, developing a practice to cultivate these traits will be essential to one's ability to navigate the landscapes with mastery.

Moments of Truth: Putting It to Practice

> *War is about long periods of boredom punctuated by moments of terror.*
>
> Unknown

Life is about moments. And so is leadership. Leaders do not "lead" every moment of the day. Exceptional leaders are often very busy, yet, quite some time passes before leadership is called upon, and then, suddenly, a challenge arises, a decision is required, or an action is called for and a leader must rise to a *moment of truth*. In the early years of SAS airlines, Jan Carlson built an entire end-to-end service concept on the notion of "*moments of truth*" – those moments of critical frontline engagement with customers. We would like to borrow the notion of a critical moment but apply *moments of truth* to those moments when leadership must stand out – the moments when a wider repertoire must be accessed to deal with a situation in the most powerful ways possible. Our device for supporting leaders to deal with moments of truth is twofold: first the ability to reorient to the landscape where energy and attention are needed, and second, the consciousness to respond with equanimity and grace to any challenge, block, or fork in the road.

Consider that we are conscious of moments because time and timing matters but not necessarily in the literal sense of a "second" or a "minute" of time. Those *moments of truth* could be a real moment, such as when news breaks or someone walks through the door with an unforeseen announcement. They might also be longer periods of time – hours, days, or even weeks, when you and your team are working through challenging situations. We will continue to refer to the idea of a "moment" to stay with one metaphor, but keep this surgeon's warning in mind.

For a leader, it is crucial to recognize the moment. It is the moment (or period) in which not only leadership is needed, but also expected. It is the occasion in which the (formal) leader can demonstrate her or his leadership, because sometimes there is no second chance to show it at that most powerful moment. Surely, a leader can recover from a missed moment, but it never matches up to being a leader in the moment when leadership is called for. Such opportunities to demonstrate leadership can be in immediate reactions to unexpected surprises yet can just as easily happen to be interventions that have been long planned. For example, when a leader announces a new strategy (which would generally be a well-planned event), does (s)he take it as a moment to bring across the information that goes with it, or does (s)he recognize it as a *moment of truth*, that calls for the leader to build momentum to reenergize and revitalize the organization?

So, we distinguish between leadership in the main as the daily routines in a leader's life and moments when new repertoires or new frames of reference become an imperative. It is in the latter case, when the *moments of truth* happens, a leader will need to be conscious of where energies and efforts are put, while sustaining dynamic balance, described in the *equanimity shift*, so the leader must come prepared for whatever will be faced.

To bring this alive, let us look at a few *moments of truth* when leaders are facing a challenge, or responding to a new situation, so we can see what determines whether or not the balanced leadership shows up powerfully. And as these *moments of truth* often come as a surprise, we will reflect on how leaders practice to be prepared for the unexpected.

7.1 Recognizing Moments of Truth

How do we know when we are in a *moment of truth*? If it is indeed *moments of truth* that matter, if it is then that your leadership will be called upon, we must first learn how to identify these moments. How do you know that you have moved from leadership in the main to a *moment of truth*? When do you know that, at this precise moment, your leadership is essential to the situation?

In the most general terms, we have established that the moments occur:

▶ when you are (individually, as a team, or as an organization as a whole) potentially disoriented about the landscape you are on or where you need to be, and/or

▶ when you (individually, as a team, or as an organization as a whole) fall out of equanimity.

Remember we spoke of *seeing*, *being*, and *doing* as the three leadership perspectives we work from? It is when you, your team, and/or your organization are challenged – unable to see the way forward on the *seeing* dimension, or when you, your team, and/or your organization are challenged about where to put your powerful energies and presence – on the *being* and *doing* dimension.

With this realization in place, you will still need one more ingredient to be equipped to recognize the moment. For that sense to develop, you must learn how to tap into the most powerful source of information you carry with you: your feelings. Because both type of moments typically go with a consciousness of your emotional state, whether it be disorientation, fear, mistrust, joy, or satisfaction. Once you learn to recognize these states, you have empowered yourself with a strong sensing device to recognize your *moments of truth*.

This naturally leads to the question "What is the recipe then for dealing with *moments of truth*." Here we must provide another surgeon's warning: there is no single recipe. There is practice in the anticipation of moments. What? No recipe? What kind of management self-help book is this? Let us explain through the eyes of the man who invented the "ignosecond."

Perhaps you have heard of a nanosecond or picosecond, but have you ever heard of an ignosecond? Most likely you have not, as this is (or was ...) a newly developed word, discovered and described by Rich Hall,[1] an American comedian and writer. In fact, he invented a whole range of new words he called "sniglets."[2] A sniglet is "any word that doesn't appear in the dictionary, but should." It is an imaginative word that covers a situation for which no existing word is well-enough suited. In his masterful collections, Hall introduces the ignosecond as "the length of time between some irretrievable action and the time you realize the consequences of that action," or "the moment of clarity just after a bone-headed act." Typically illustrated by the moment you realize you left your keys inside the car with all doors locked, that lengthy moment when everything stands still between letting go of the car door and hearing it slam close. It might be the ignosecond when you realize you have just addressed your partner with the name of your previous partner or when you are talking to a client and refer to the competitor's company in your example rather than his company. We will let your imagination run wild with all the situations and their potentially devastating consequences. But what have ignoseconds got to do with *moments of truth*?

We use the ignosecond to illustrate the impact our default behaviors can have at any moment in time. While we cannot provide you with a recipe to deal with every *moment of truth*, we do advocate sharpening your response system through practices. Before we jump into practices, let us look at a few more examples of the devastating effect of missing opportunities to respond to Moments Of Truth because of our unconscious auto-pilot behavior. In a large scale leadership development session we recently designed and led, we invited the CEO of a 50,000+ people organization to meet with a group of 25 senior leaders. The purpose was to exchange perspectives in a one hour dialogue. The company had recently announced a number of strategic activities, of which one was "a better alignment of its leadership potential." Needless to say this included making a number of people redundant. The buzz among the top group was that this would affect about 10 percent of senior management.

Naturally, this was a topic of discussion, and at some point, the CEO was challenged with the question whether he realized he was introducing fear into the organization. He responded in an unconscious way that did exactly what he was being accused of; in his verbal and non-verbal answer he addressed and challenged the questioner in an aggressive way. In addition, several hours after the dialogue, the individual who raised the question was summoned to come by his office as soon as the session was finished. The bewildered manager shared his worries with his colleagues, which added to the existing perception of management by fear.

It is at moments such as this, when leaders are unexpectedly questioned on their actions (hence: faced with a new situation) that our equanimity-across-the-landscapes repertoire comes to play or not. The CEO took the comment on the Individual/personal Landscape, and therefore felt attacked about his integrity and leadership. He did not have the presence of mind to quickly reframe the challenge to a wider landscape, otherwise he might have been able to explain the measures he took in the light of the changes he witnessed in the industry or the improvements he wanted to bring about on the *organizational landscape*, thereby shifting it from the limited perspective of the *individual landscape*. In the blink of an eye he might have reframed the perspective and left his top leaders with the feeling: "Now that's why he's the leader."

To pick up the thread of the *equanimity shift*, he had not (yet) mastered *recovery*. Being pushed offbalance by this perceived personal attack, he might have chosen to take three conscious breaths to deal with the internal anxiety that gripped him. Or he might have used humor to recover the moment, catch his breath, and move to a more powerful choice of responses.

It is these recovery techniques that guide us back to dynamic balance, that shift us back to equanimity, so we can use the other dimensions of equanimity to enact our leadership mastery. In the case described, *presence* is the attribute that comes into focus, as it is was through his *presence* in facing this situation that he might have established his leadership credibility. But to be present he first needed to become conscious of the landscape to recover from the perceived attack.

7.2   Rising to the leadership challenge in our Moments of Truth

Moments of truth come in many shapes and forms. They have in common that they are moments/periods when one is facing a (new) situation. Typical examples of such moments are:

▶ When you need to face up to a crisis
▶ When acknowledgment and celebration is called for
▶ When pivotal news needs to be announced/communicated
▶ When a decision needs to be made before other things can happen.

They cover situations that can be prepared for (e.g. the announcement of a restructuring) and situations for which one cannot be prepared (e.g. being faced with a sudden crisis). Yet, despite these archetypes of moments, or classifications of particular situations, we must again acknowledge that there is no one recipe for dealing with each situation. Facing up to a crisis can come in many shapes and forms, some that require immediate action, others that require significant time to reflect and temporize. As Adair established many years ago in his landmark book on situational leadership[3] "every new situation brings its own set of conditions." As he suggests and as we advocate, it is the recombinant logic that matters. And the recombinant components we offer to deal with *moments of truth* are in the details of our two pillars, orienting on one's *leadership landscapes* and regaining balance through an *equanimity shift.*

Below we will show in some more detail how these two ideas – navigating landscapes and balancing through equanimity – dance with one another to produce powerful, responsive leadership for almost every situation. Perhaps a simple way to enter into this conversation is this: powerful leaders have the capacity to see more, be more, and do more in the service of others.

7.2.1   SEEING

Situations where leadership is required to see more are usually rational challenges and typically deal with sense making against the background of complexity. In these situations *leadership landscapes* as well as the attributes *"eye for possibility"* and *"reframing"* come to the foreground.

In our current times, for instance, globalization and technological advances, to name just two, have had a tremendous effect on how business is run, adding new dimensions of uncertainty and possibility to the palette of choices and decisions. In addition to these broadened perspectives comes the speed in which change follows through. The perception of Asia in recent years illustrates how fast perspectives change and matter on a global scale. In 2003 Asia was largely tainted by the fear of avian flu; hotels throughout Asia had to close their doors as a result of total absence of business as Asia was perceived as "dangerous." Within two years, India and China have become the challengers of the world economy. That is how fast it can go nowadays, with ever decreasing barriers to shift business variables – such as production, knowledge work, and capitalization – across the globe.

Amidst all that is the leader who is charged with providing a path forward, a perspective that is comprehensible and energizing, one that does justice to the complexity, while maintaining a coherent and simple-enough message to the whole of the organization. It is the leader's role to navigate across the landscapes and reframe perspectives, so that sense making can take place with the whole integrated picture in mind. It is no use picking off the easy targets or going for the low hanging fruit if the result is a greater complexity that arises from the unintended consequences of such actions.

So the art of *seeing*, for a busy executive, can be likened to a laser beam that pulls all of the light together into a coherent and powerful form. To make it work requires coherence. Communicating coherence means mastering one's ability to gain a *perspective* across the Landscapes, and therefore being able to see things in an *integrated* fashion. At the same time, without a practiced mindset of equanimity, a busy executive will not take time to cultivate an *eye for possibility*, a precondition for *reframing* any situation he or she may face.

7.2.2 BEING

Other *moments of truth* draw on who you are as a leader, as an individual actor. Where do you draw the line on an ethical dilemma? Where do you stand on points of principle? Which developments do you encourage, which cultures and values do you nurture, which behaviors do you tolerate, and not tolerate?

In these *moments of truth* it is essential that leaders will have reflected on the Equanimity attribute that draws attention to one's *enduring commitments*. Sustained enduring commitments and deep intentions provide dynamic balance and energy that will allow you to perform on a mentally sustainable level. It is the legacy you want to leave behind as a leader in the organization, so one day you can say, referring back to our earlier quote from a "Level 5" leader interviewed by Jim Collins: "I want to look out from my porch at one of the great companies in the world someday and be able to say, 'I used to work there.'"[4] But those who are now sitting on their porches will tell you that getting to that point may have been simple, but it was not easy. They probably had to work through a host of moments when they were torn apart by competing commitments and worn down by competing values that challenged their own enduring commitments. Yet the leaders that rise above the others find a way to hold on to their enduring commitments and weave them into the stories of their lives and work. We all know of stories about those who did not adhere to their strong values and commitments. The Buddhists liken our commitments to an "axis mundi" of our lives, a sort of maypole around which all things circle.

Finally, a leader's ability to have the equanimity to sustain *presence* and be present in any situation, where they are, has the magical ability, when performed well, to transform nearly any complex uneasy situation into an opportunity to reassure and to put actions into context. As Professor Erik van de Loo of INSEAD insists: "On a base level, leaders are for their teams, and their organization, the people who contain fear, give us perspective, and draw us to the situation at hand."

7.2.3   DOING

There is a school of thought that came long before the Nike epithet "Just Do It!". Some board members at a team meeting in Dubai recently exclaimed "JFDI" (we will leave this acronym to your imagination) to their troops, so one board member JFDI'd some bribes to public officials in a hurry to win competitive contracts and pulled the whole company into a tailspin. Yes, leadership is always, on some level, about doing. Leaders in most roles are expected, above all, to be people of action. While this is true for most leaders, we counter such a notion by suggesting that many decisions beyond the day-to-day variety happen when the time is right. David Kreuzer, a remarkable systems thinker from Massachusetts Institute of Technology once said: "Sometimes we say to leaders: 'Don't just stand there, do something!' but in many cases, we should be saying: 'Don't just do something, stand there!' " Dynamic balance is therefore as much about your ability to hold your action as it is to act immediately.

Timing of action also matters because we don't have endless amounts of energy available, and we must therefore be ready to play when the time is right, not too early nor too late. This is an awareness that is very much apparent with athletes, who not only worry about being in top shape on time, but also know not to peak too early. Peaking too early is as damaging as peaking too late in sports and so it is as well in leadership. It is also true in the arts. Henri Cartier-Bresson (1908–2005) became famous for his photographs of Parisian street scenes: lovers kissing, a child proudly smiling between two bottles of wine. He defined this ability to capture " "the decisive moment," when "the simultaneous recognition, in a fraction of a second, of the significance of an event as well as the precise organisation of forms...gives that event its proper expression."[5] The lesson for leaders is clear: a sense of timing when it comes to decisions can mean the difference between a meaningful expression of effort and completion of an empty act.

Perhaps we all know when our timing was off or when we missed the boat. Many will remember the scene of an American president, sitting in a classroom of grade school kids, when a colleague whispered that a horrible situation would require his immediate attention. In his role as Commander in Chief, he remained seated for a remarkably long time before getting up to act. He may have been conflicted about the need to support his brother's election campaign or he may have been considering the affairs of state. Either way, he froze, and seemed genuinely unable to act on the news that was whispered in his ear.[6] This was an irreversible moment when leadership was required, yet his *recovery* mechanisms, as well as his *eye for possibility* most probably left him, and the nation saw a leader who was not able to react to the one situation that defined his presidency.

Stepping up to the *moments of truth* is not an option for leaders, it's a must.

TOWARD MASTERY

Toward Mastery: How to Do This?

In the quest to define and develop talent in international companies, two myths have gained general acceptance:

1. There is a war for talent.
2. Every one needs to overcome their gaps according to the competence profile, capability profile, or whatever convenient name the consultants have christened it.

The war for talent, developed by McKinsey and company in the early 21st century framed the talent pipeline in the following way: "Demographics suggest that companies will fall radically short of their needs for skilled professionals in the next 10–15 years. Therefore, gear up to grab talent from competitors, and where there are persistent gaps, call us." The report had the immediate effect of producing numerous conferences on the subject and inflating the price of scarce talent. It only confirmed the suspicions of the really good talent that, if they were to succeed, they would ultimately have to make their own way, carefully supported by a few invisible champions and carefully selected, well-timed visits to blue-chip business schools for "tune-ups."

Unfortunately nobody bothered to ask the most essential question: if this is our strategy and purpose as a company, what sort of mastery will we need? Talent and mastery are tricky chicken and egg ideas.

8.1 Mastery

It was 7:15 and a man in martial arts clothing was going through his paces in the first light of the day in the courtyard of a castle in Mello, about 100 km north of Paris. By 8:00 sounds could be heard that could only come from an expression of inner spirit externalized through boost of energies. By 8:15 he was in full flow, wiping his broomstick through the air against imaginary aggressors on all sides. And at 8:30, he had brought his practice to a gradual end, and was resting, with his eyes closed, in total balance and harmony, physically and mentally.

What happened next was nothing short of utterly remarkable. Twenty-three senior financial service professional gathered around him and formed a circle, and on his command they began to slowly undulate their bodies, making wide circles with their pelvis. "Imagine the orb at the centre of your pelvis.... Slowly move it around in a circle." By the end of a half week of practice, as a part of one of our *leadership landscapes* leadership programs, the group had learned some essential Aikido terminology and moves. They had mastered some of the starting techniques of this graceful form of martial arts. But more important, they had observed and learned from a 7th Dan Aikido master and understood that mastery is a whole person concept that relies on the corps/body memory as much as on the brain. That visualizing is essential to enacting and that sometimes being is as important as doing.

When we speak of *mastery*, we frame it as a journey, a quest, in which the object of the exercise is continuous practice to refine this practice in holistic ways.

When Aikido masters or dancers isolate parts of a motion done by their body, the intention is to focus and refine the motion in order to then reintegrate it back into a combination of moves that adds up to a performance. This was discovered already by John O'Neil,[1] in his landmark book *"Leadership Aikido."* There is no such thing as Taylorism in Aikido. No division of labor and specialization on a specific point. It is all integrated. As a metaphor, this works for business in permanent fast forward, as a way to think about our work across the landscapes. It is no longer useful to dwell on gaps.

I learned this difference in 1994, when I worked with Henri Mintzberg and the late Sumantra Ghoshal on the creation of a leadership program for the development of the next leaders we wanted to have in the organization at Shell. Until then I had, as a young HR professional, always worked in the traditional way of human development: we would develop competence frameworks for our senior management and identify the ideal competencies we would need to meet the next level of challenges. Subsequently, the question always became: "how do we shore up the gap between where we want our leaders to be, and where they are today?" After we had worked our way through identifying the inspirational levels, Sumantra Ghoshal – who I respected tremendously – went right at it, and suggested a starting angle into the program we were designing together: "So, in our workshop, what we must ask these leaders is, 'why aren't you good enough?' " Ghoshal, as a strategic thinker, was steeped in the school of resource-based strategy, effectively leading him to approach a problem from the perspective of what are the competencies needed to meet the challenges of the future we face.

Henri Mintzberg disagreed with him however. Coming from a world in which he tried to understand what was in the mind of leaders, and always contemplating on how one could tap into the wisdom and inspiration everyone holds inside oneself, he stated that that was the wrong question to ask. He said: "What we should ask instead is: what have you done that is remarkable and great in any theater of your life? And what do we need to do to bring that into Shell?"

In a flash, I understood the difference between competency gaps and mastery.

8.2 Practice

As you read these lines, we encourage you to ask yourself how you make sense of them, how you have mastered this skill of reading words, and making sense of them in your head. Your obvious answer to this question might be that you "learned to do this at school." Which is probably true. But just going to school by itself teaches you nothing, the school is merely a building, an institution, in which a framework for learning is provided. So, there must be more. How about this: "My teacher taught me how to read." Again, this is probably true at some level, but it still does not explain how you have mastered it. So, what, really, is it that leads you to mastery? As you might have to draw on what appears to be an ancient past, think about something you have mastered in more recent times. Maybe you have recently learned how to sail a boat, how to fly an airplane, or how to cook classic Chinese meals. Either way, did you master those skills by simply listening to the teacher? Surely not. The teacher was there to provide the instructions and subsequently provide the boundaries to your experimentation (or in the case of flight instructions, the boundary to your disaster). The actual learning to master skills comes through practice.

The same goes for learning in your business environment today. Nothing has changed in how you master a new skill from the days you left the school benches. If anything has changed, it is that the stakes are now much higher and the cost of failure much bigger. Therefore it is amazing that, in many ways, we have lost the art of practice. Or at least we have mostly become alienated from the idea, as adults.

That is why we aim to bring practice back into a leader's life, as we strongly believe practice is vital in taking on some of these new ideas.

Think of something you did well when you were young. Even those skills that you feel you have already acquired require further practice. They get rusty, or they run stale, so there is a continuous need for refreshment. Therefore, besides bringing back practice as a proven personal development technique, we also want to undo the myth that practice is only for the novice. If you think a once acquired skill remains fresh for a lifetime, think again. In that sense, skills are just like fashion. Just look at a picture of yourself 15 years ago; you would not be wearing those clothes today, would you?

An MBA teacher at a European university once told us the story of Gregg, a 27-year-old MBA student. As part of the strategy curriculum, students engaged in a number of case studies and presented their findings to the rest of the group. Every week another group would present, and the teacher had succeeded in putting the bar of expectation at a very high level. So, this was a fun and exciting experience for all, but at the same token it was nerve racking and stressful to most of the students as well. But not to Gregg, who was a confident, well-spoken New Yorker, with a charming personality, a warm voice, and a beautiful smile. Besides being a natural speaker, he had the advantage of being the result of an education system where making presentations was an integral part in learning (contrary to most European schools). And of course, English was his mother tongue (which was not the case for 80 percent of the other students). So presenting his group's findings was not a major concern to him.

Always arriving 15 minutes prior to the start of the class, the teacher had gotten used to finding the presenters there, putting the final hand on their presentation, generally overstressing themselves more than needed. It was not uncommon that he had to comfort and relax them a bit in those final minutes, just to ensure they "kept breathing." This morning he did not expect any of that, as he knew Gregg had volunteered to present his group's findings, and surely Gregg would come in just before, fire up his computer, and confidently take the group through what they had found.

And indeed, as he entered the classroom, it was empty, just as expected. But as he was preparing the classroom, he heard a voice from the adjacent classroom, which he knew was empty. He went to look and to his surprise he found Gregg presenting his findings to an empty room. As he was curious about this unexpected encounter, he asked "Gregg, what are you doing? I thought you were not here, and imagined you would come in just before we started." Gregg looked at him puzzled and replied: "But sir, surely I must practice – this is an opportunity for me to learn."

Here was a naturally talented presenter, who, in the face of the task and audience in front of him, could have easily gotten by drawing on his existing capabilities. Yet, he understood the value of practice and grasped the opportunity to further master his skills. That is how we become masters, using every opportunity we have to practice. Just like the famous soccer player Thierry Henry replied when he was asked what he practiced: "I work on those things I do best."

There is another significant difference between our learning as young-sters and our learning today. We do not spend most of our waking hours in a classroom setting and therefore we are not continuously encouraged to use every opportunity to learn. We challenge by asking you to reframe your notion that learning only takes place in a classroom or in an offsite environment, when we are freed from the busy-ness of our daily lives. We promote the idea that learning and mastering can take place at any moment in time and in every space you desire.

Of course you already knew this, yet we want to bring it to the fore-front of your consciousness. Our aim through *leadership landscapes* is to take individuals and organizations to the tipping point of new ways of thinking and being, and in doing so, to a transformational stage for themselves and/or their organization. We therefore provide five power-ful practices that you can build into your work and daily lives that will directly work to sharpen your edges and mastery, especially as it refers to the *leadership landscapes perspective* and the *equanimity shift*. They vary in their degree of "technique-ness," their time consumption, and their focus, yet all give you sound, practical ideas on how you can reach mastery. All are useful and are done by many leaders across many fields whom we work with today.

We do not intend to merely provide some powerful insights with our perspective on how the pieces of leadership fit together, we also encourage you to work on your own mastery skills by adopting these practices. All are straightforward, proven approaches that will have direct impact on your performance as a leader. Surely, our set cannot be complete, and there are other things we apply and promote – yet these five have been selected to give you the most powerful headstart in developing your full potential for leadership.

8.3   Practice 1: Landscape balancing diagnostic

Our starting practice is one that establishes the ground work for how you engage with the landscapes. We provide a diagnostic toolset that works from the simple observation of how you spend your time on each of the landscapes, and what your natural tendencies (or defaults) are, at http://www.leadershiplandscapes.com.

Knowing how you and your team spend your time is immediately valuable. Do you cover the whole spectrum of what is relevant for you? Are you overfocusing on the burning issues on one or two landscapes? Can you broaden your horizons by consciously building in time spent on landscapes you do not frequently visit? These are valuable questions that can be answered by first establishing your common ground: how do I typically spend my time and where do I put my energy? It reveals a lot about how you might be approaching the issues you face.

With that in mind there are a few balancing acts that come into play. With your knowledge of how you spend your time, we acknowledge that surely, there is no "right" proportion of time – or leadership attention units (LAUs) – to be spent at each level. This will largely depend on factors such as industry, role, state of the organization, and more. Yet, it does pay off to establish if time is spent in balance. Definitely, if it becomes apparent that one or more landscapes consistently get ignored, there is balancing work to do.

The other balancing act to play is how the time spent across the landscapes matches or mismatches your natural skills and behavioral defaults. Are there significant gaps between how you actually spend your time across the landscapes and where your natural interests lie? These gaps may not be immediately problematic, but if they are sustained over time they will undoubtedly impact your effectiveness as a leader. We can resist our natural preferences for some time, but we cannot ignore them. Especially as leadership in the face of the changing business environment becomes more demanding, the ongoing misfit between how we would prefer to spend our time compared to how we do spend our time becomes unsustainable.

This takes us to the third balancing act to consider: how are the LAUs of your team distributed? This is more than the aggregate of the individual spending, yet the aggregate provides a starting point. Just as a football team cannot function when it consists of only defenders or attackers, or even worse, only left-field defenders, the leadership team as a whole must enact a similar diversity in their landscape coverage.

To see how this diagnostic quickly sheds light on the leadership team composition, their defaults, and their actual time spending, have a look at some profiles we took from a team of executives we worked with in the financial industry:

Leader 1 shows a remarkably high score on actual time spent on the organization landscape, while her natural interests are clearly more on the industry and markets landscape (Figure 8.1). It is a common profile found with leaders that are temporarily – or structurally – involved in "too many" internally oriented activities, such as reorganizations, managing IT projects, handling rationalization processes, and so on, at the costs of what brought them to what they really enjoy: working with customers. A profile like leader 1 is not problematic, as long as it is temporary. Although even during this temporary phase one can wonder whether this is the right person in the right place. Yet, if this is a structural profile, and maybe even part of the job the leader is given, this will undoubtedly become an issue, and surely this person is placed in an unsustainable role.

Leader 2 shows a similar pattern, with again some significant gaps between natural interests and actual time spent (Figure 8.2). This profile is actually quite typical in that we find it a lot in executive teams.

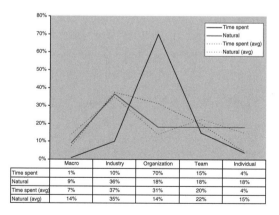

	Macro	Industry	Organization	Team	Individual
Time spent	1%	10%	70%	15%	4%
Natural	9%	36%	18%	18%	18%
Time spent (avg)	7%	37%	31%	20%	4%
Natural (avg)	14%	35%	14%	22%	15%

Figure 8.1   Landscape Profile Leader 1

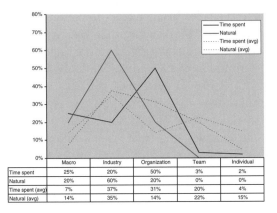

	Macro	Industry	Organization	Team	Individual
Time spent	25%	20%	50%	3%	2%
Natural	20%	60%	20%	0%	0%
Time spent (avg)	7%	37%	31%	20%	4%
Natural (avg)	14%	35%	14%	22%	15%

Figure 8.2   Landscape Profile Leader 2

How would you typify it? We call it the "salesman"-type; it is people who have very strong interests on the industry landscape (quite often, the customer/commercial process), and relatively low interests in other land-scapes. Clearly, commercial success is often a impetus to move up the lad-der in the organization. Yet those upper hierarchy-roles also imply more attention on the organization landscapes, as seniors get more involved in issues such as governance, staffing, and budgets.

Leader 2 has another remarkable characteristic in his profile: the absence of the individual landscape both in natural interest as well as in actual time spent. The balancing act on this profile is not so much align-ing the two (as they are already aligned near 0), but working through the implications of a leader who does not appear to underwrite the need for personal development and maintenance.

Leader 3 showed a remarkably, and rather rare, very close alignment between the natural interest and actual time spent (Figure 8.3). It is rare to find such a close alignment.

8.3.1   LEADERSHIP LANDSCAPES DEFAULT BEHAVIOR

So we get to the fundamental question: if we were to identify our natural interests, or defaults, how would we sustain dynamic balance if our time spending – based on our role in the organization – is not aligned with our natural interests? This is of course an intriguing question and the answer is not straightforward. Clearly, step 1 is to identify the defaults and time actually spent, as without acknowledgement there is no way forward. Coming to realize that you are – probably unconsciously – maintaining

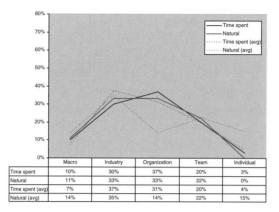

	Macro	Industry	Organization	Team	Individual
Time spent	10%	30%	37%	20%	3%
Natural	11%	33%	33%	22%	0%
Time spent (avg)	7%	37%	31%	20%	4%
Natural (avg)	14%	35%	14%	22%	15%

Figure 8.3   Landscape Profile Leader 3

gaps between your time spent and your natural interests is a major achievement, a valuable insight to start developing yourself.

However, if they are not in line, there are no easy answers. Some situations are clearly worse than others. If the mismatch is of a temporary nature, it will most likely not lead to a significant problem. Humans are generally strong and flexible enough to deal with such mismatches. If it is however of a structural nature, what can be done? Clearly, there is the solution of the last resort, which would be to seek a different role. That is not where we start, but bear in mind that it might be your conclusion in the end. Fortunately there is a lot to do before that comes into view.

We do not support the traditional way human resource development deals with gaps. Traditionally, the focus is on the laggards, and defining a development path that intends to work on those specifically. With the intent and hope that the lagging edges can be brought up to a level that closes the mismatch. We fundamentally disagree with this perspective for a number of reasons, not in the least because it is going against human nature.

What we propose is to use the master tool to ignite creativity in dealing with the challenges one faces. By broadening the perspective, one will find that solutions to problems that at first seem to lie conventionally within a particular landscape can often be found at a different landscape. In particular, landscapes that draw your most natural interests and are connected to your *enduring commitment* are a great source for uncovering unconventional solutions to issues you face.

In order to engage in "landscape broadening" as we call it, we provide a technique called *inquiry mapping*, which is the subject of our next practice.

8.4   Practice 2: Inquiry mapping

Once you start working with the landscapes, how do you build an active understanding of them? And how do you make them work to solve real, practical problems that you face? Most landscapes are more complex than they may seem when first appraised and, until they have been studied a bit, dramatic action may be premature and have the effect of squandering rather than building the credibility and legitimacy required for sustained leadership. But how do you sort through the wilderness of competing demands for attention and action to set your priorities and acting? And how can you do it in a practical way, without the need to outsource it to others? Effectively, how do you create a rich understanding of an issue at hand and/or solve a real problem in an integrated fashion by using the landscapes and with the least drain on your LAUs?

The criteria for an approach that helps you deal with the landscapes would then be that it is first and foremost practical, not too time-consuming, that it can be applied independently and individually, that it provides integrated answers and actions, and simplifies, but not oversimplifies, your complexity. *inquiry mapping* provides a lot toward these ends. It is a generic way of identifying and assessing possibilities, risks, and opportunities to a full enough degree to do justice to the inherent complexity of things – and to see connections that reveal what might otherwise take you by surprise. Because using this tool allows you to see the relations among multiple issues, you make decisions about priorities and allocate time and resources more judiciously.

Moreover, *inquiry mapping* is a practical tool for untangling seemingly intractable sets of problems and for taking fresh approaches to seemingly irreconcilable dilemmas. It is a way of seeing the relations among things with a tool that is simple enough to use yet sophisticated enough to be useful at a very high level.

When you are focusing on a landscape, say the *industry landscape* (but it suits for all landscapes) you need to be thinking of the most important dimensions at hand. This is how to come to a truly multidimensional map of the landscape territory and capture rich insights about the issue.

Let us examine how this works by creating an *inquiry map*. Typically, you would use a whiteboard or flipcharts for this. It will work well with one to six people at a time, so it can be useful for individual or team work.

8.4.1   STEP 1: DISCOVER ISSUES

The first stage of creating an *inquiry map* is the process of deciding on the issues that need to be addressed, assuming you are not using it for a specific problem at hand (if you are applying it for a specific problem at hand, this step is simplified as that is your issue – yet, do spend time deciding in what landscape your problem naturally sits).

Before you construct your *inquiry map*, spend time in group conversation to bring out the issues and problems that you want to confront. Ask yourself/your group very open questions and bring out all that seems to matter or relate to this issue.

Inevitably this will throw up a series of things that may lie in quite different categories: from individuals' issues within teams to, say, strategic problems with international distribution. The important thing is to let the conversation be as wide-ranging as possible and to gather all the issues and problems as frankly as possible.

8.4.2   STEP 2: CLUSTER PER LANDSCAPE

We will quickly see that while most issues will naturally fall into one landscape or another, some may show up on more than one. Cluster your issues, first per landscape – duplicate issues if they cover more than one landscape. Ideally use sticky notes (e.g. post-its) to cluster.

8.4.3   STEP 3: CREATE DIMENSIONS

Now, choose the landscape that you want to deepen. This would normally be the landscape with the most relevant or immediate challenges. As you can repeat this step for each landscape, it is not critical that you choose the "right" landscape. Yet in terms of prioritizing your efforts, focus on what matters most to you first.

Next, within a landscape, cluster the issues that were brought up into four categories. Each of these categories stands as a dimensional subset of that particular landscape. In *inquiry mapping* we always work with *four* dimensions, for reasons that will become apparent shortly.

Having chosen one of these sets of four issues, we need to lay them out on our *inquiry map*. The default shape of an *inquiry map* is as follows.

For example, say, our categories on the Organization Landscape are the following:

▶ structure
▶ processes/systems
▶ values/culture
▶ people.

Our first *inquiry map* then becomes:

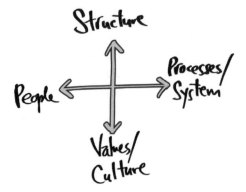

8.4.4   STEP 4: DISCUSS DIMENSIONS AND RELATIONS

The bulk of the session should be spent discussing each area in depth and specifying the mutual impacts of each issue to each other issue. As you have typically already explored the individual dimensions in the previous step (you have, after all, clustered them into your dimensions), shift the discussion to how the different dimensions impact each other. Say, we start from the dimension "Structure." Explore first how "Structure" and "Values/culture" are related. Capture the discussion, so you have a good understanding of how these two pivotal dimensions are related.

Next, discuss how "Structure" and "Processes/systems" are related. Repeat this for "Structure" and "People." When finished, you now have a rich view of how Structure is related to the other issues that matter on the Organization Landscape.

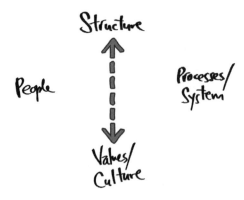

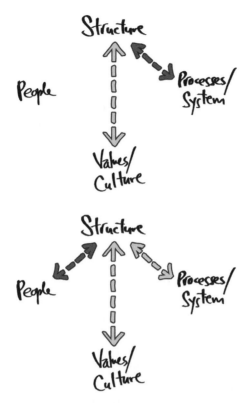

When continuing this process for the other relationships, we uncover 3 more relationships: "People" with "Processes/Systems," "People" with "Values/Culture," and finally "Processes/Systems" with "Values/ Culture," as represented by the figure below:

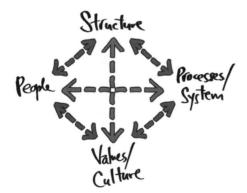

Having gone through this exercise, you will have deepened and explored the landscape by addressing in depth the key dimensions as well as their inter-relationships.

8.4.5   WHY INQUIRY MAPPING?

Inquiry mapping is a rich and integrated way to approach a landscape. Any effective way of dealing with complex issues requires a level of abstraction and reduction; the challenge is not to lose too much information in your narrowing approach. One typical pitfall in other approaches is that the categories (or dimensions) are analyzed in further detail *without* paying conscious attention to how they relate to the other key dimensions identified. These approaches do not acknowledge the inherently integrated nature of complex issues – we therefore propose to explicitly visit the inter-relationships as a way to resolve tensions and visualize interdependent and mutual possibilities.

A common question is, why should I use four dimensions, and not three or five or even more. The answer is that *inquiry mapping* is aimed at providing a sufficient level of clarity into complex matters. This means that any approach must provide clarity (hence: reduce complexity), yet not oversimplify. Also, it has to acknowledge that things are complex because they (often) come with a large set of inter-relationships, sometimes obvious, but very often hidden. By enforcing four dimensions, we bring out ten points of entry to the Landscape: the four chosen dimensions, and their six relationships. More dimensions would not reduce the complexity (e.g. five dimensions give fifteen angles, which rapidly becomes too much), less dimensions would oversimplify inherently complex matters (e.g. three dimensions would give 6 angles). Practically, we have therefore found four dimensions to work best to facilitate a powerful and insightful, yet not dragging exploration.

8.4.6   OPTIONAL EXTENSIONS

Some optional extensions to *inquiry mapping* can be useful:

Weighing Relationships – Once mutual impacts have been specified, it is useful to weigh the relationships between dimensions. Some links are always likely to stand out for greater interest, more accessible intervention points or more likely results. This approach can be useful, but we warn that this should not be applied by default, as it introduces the risk of overlooking or underestimating the impact of links, which could emerge from the exploration.

Off-shooting Dimensions – Each individual dimension of the *inquiry map* can be further explored with its own *inquiry map*. This can be useful when it becomes clear that the categorization that led to the dimension has brought it at such high level, that too much information has been lost. At that point you can choose to off-shoot a dimension, and explore it again with its own *inquiry map*, as shown below:

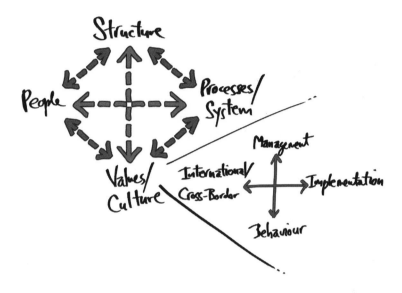

8.4.7 EXAMPLES OF INQUIRY MAPPING AND POWERFUL DIMENSIONS

For illustration, let us look at several *inquiry maps*. We emphasize however that these just serve as examples – there are no hard rules to what your dimensions should be. This is situational, and – in our experience – easily found by following the approach we suggest above.

We have grouped our examples per landscape. On the *individual landscape*, a particularly useful set of dimensions we have found in our role as executive coaches are the following:

1. **Meaning** – how you make meaning and find purpose in your life and work, your enduring commitments, your sense of calling and spirit.
2. **Work** – the leadership context, challenges, and immediate projects at hand.
3. **Life's Contours and Balances** – your life story, interests outside of work, the realm of domestic life and key relationships, issues of energy, health and vitality, and so on.
4. **Material Needs** – are the necessary means available to support your leadership projects and work as well as your life beyond your work (what are your material needs)?

On the *team landscape*, useful dimensions to consider are as follows:

1. **Purpose** – what is this team's purpose and remit?
2. **Composition** – who is on the team, what are their roles in the organization, and what role does each play on the team?
3. **Skills and competencies** – what characteristics and attributes does each individual bring to the team?
4. **Behaviors and personalities** – How does each team member act and how does the team as a whole behave?

For the *organizational landscape,* a useful set of dimensions could be the ones used in the example above, being:

1. Structure – Hierarchy, flat, matrix?
2. Processes/systems – Technologies, process steps? Roles?
3. Values and culture – Evolving? Loose? Tight? Explicit?
4. People – Behaviours? Competencies? Skills? Knowledge?

At the Landscape of **Industry and Markets**, useful dimensions could be:

1. Competition – Five forces? Consolidating? Leading? Lagging?
2. Customers – Brand awareness? Segments? B2B? B2C?
3. Suppliers – Integrated? Many? Few? Sourcing strategy?
4. Stakeholders – Importance? Supportive? Combative?

Or possibly dimensions such as Innovation, Profitability, or International.
Finally, at the landscape level of **Macro-business,** you could array issues such as

1. Political and Regulatory – Stable? Changing? Heavy? Light?
2. Economic – Supportive Climate? Drivers? International relationships?
3. Technological/environmental – Speed of change? IP ownership?
4. Social/cultural – Business supports? Priorities?

8.4.8 WHY IS THIS TECHNIQUE ANY DIFFERENT FROM JUST BRAINSTORMING OR OTHER WORKSHOP TOOLS?

Brainstorming can be a useful tool for generating content but it frequently results in a sort of wish-list which has both discarded other important issues and has reduced problems or issues into "discrete categories." We feel strongly that the real issues are often *between* the categories. The lists that come out of brainstorming sessions are frequently difficult to take forward. They are what we call New Year's Resolution Lists, full of good intention but with little context or strategy available and often important bits of the story are missing.

Inquiry mapping's central virtue is that it helps us make relationships within a larger whole explicit. It does this by asking us to consider how each component of a whole impacts each of the other components.

Other techniques are often divisively incomplete or difficult to use. *Inquiry mapping* is a gift. It is a mobile, simple, and practical tool you can carry about in your head. It is a unique approach to inquiry solving. It allows us not simply to "solve" problems but to approach them and understand them. One consequence of this is a different understanding of strategic thinking. Inevitably we have found this approach to lead us to longer term realities and perspectives. Although immediate problems, realities, and outcomes are important, they will often be able to be seen in a wider frame after successful *inquiry mapping* across the landscapes.

This is the function of the simple *inquiry map* structure in our practice. It is the practical embodiment of our larger message, which is to be able to see in the round, to be able to see further and deeper into the issues that confront us, and to be able to weigh the available options and implications.

Of course computers and networks can work out sets of issues and their relations to the "n-th" degree but the beauty of the *inquiry mapping* system is that it is "visual thinking," it encapsulates and facilitates a practice that is creative, shared, and public. By exploring the issues and constructing the *inquiry map*, participants are joining in a shared practice, a creative dialogue, and it is through this process itself that the relation between seemingly intractable problems and new possible answers can be seen.

8.5   Practice 3: The Reflective Moment

Where our previous practices typically focused on using and exploring the *leadership landscape* model, we now refer to practices that extend your leadership capacity along the dimensions of our Equanimity Model. Our third practice is of a different order. It is a conscious practice that helps you in sense making, hence working on your ability to Reframe, sharpen your *eye for possibility*, and improve your capacity to Recover and improve your *presence*.

It is the practice of "*The reflective moment.*" Reflection is the only way to consciously integrate your experience into your behavior. If you do not have a reflective practice you are learning by chance without harvesting learning from what you are doing and the tendency to repeat the same mistakes over and over becomes virtually inevitable. The *reflective moment* assists you in being able to see the widest possible consequences and possibilities without losing sight of what is right in front of your face. It is about gaining a different perspective and integrating your experience so that you stand on terra firma with equanimity.

Our process of embodying this practice starts from where you are. And if your base – your center – is right, you can move out from it in concentric circles. The trick is not to get mired in particularist traps about your team, your division, your product, or your self, but to view all of your challenges and all of these areas of your life and work as interrelated landscapes. With a wider field of reference, you expand. This is about the grounding of what you know and the acceptance of what you do not.

Our experience of this practice is that it is in the grounding of what I know. It is not about more content – it is about asking yourself, can I consciously reflect on what we have been saying? If you can do this about this book – and you do it for other things you do for the rest of your life – you are going to weave together your practices at a much more integrated level. While reflection requires an inward glance, it is always in the service of looking upward and onward, with an enhanced consciousness of your role in the world. This is the aim of our reflective practice. It is about becoming more systematically conscious of yourself, your commitments, your roles, your intentions, your reasons, your actions, your impact, and your legacies. It represents the culmination of this book's lessons and ideas.

The first thing that we should state is that pause and reflection is an integral part of transformative growth – and to remind you that this book is about development and not about partial improvement. The *reflective moment* is that time taken to think about what's best, consider your core intentions, and to take a good long look at yourself. It is not a method devised for ongoing introspection nor informed by a therapeutic psychologism but intended as a rehearsal of the future, a platform for action, a projection forward.

We refer to it as a "moment" because it should be an inbuilt recurring aside: brief, but serious in intent. It should not be a lifetime spent on introspection. *Vivendo discimus* – by living we learn.

After surveying some of the most effective leaders across time, some of the key attributes we have outlined already stand out: the need to broaden the perspective from a mindset of equanimity in all its forms. But all of these tools and techniques are less than useless if they are not allied with a period of reflection before action. Returning to some of our exemplary leaders through whom we introduced the aspects of equanimity, each of them had developed a clear inward dimension of reflection in their life and work. And we can locate for each of them a clear practice field provided by life circumstances on which they honed this practice to a high art.

Nelson Mandela's autobiography, *Long Walk to Freedom*, is a beautiful study in the self reflections of a great man who is working to live up to his place in history in the very way he tells his story, which is full of dilemmas, youthful mischief, and the high purpose conferred by a cause for the realization of which he hoped to live but on behalf of which he was prepared to die. Mandela's developed capacity for self-reflection is evident before the trial at which he was sentenced to life imprisonment, particularly in the decision he took to lead the African National Congress (ANC) away from its commitment to exclusively non-violent means of resistance in the wake of the Sharpesville massacre, a choice requiring that he himself go underground as an outlaw.

But it was the process of writing this biography which speaks most clearly to reflection as a developed art. Mandela was forced to write his book in secret over many years of imprisonment, during which he was often placed in solitary confinement. For him, the replaying of the past and the refining of its sensibilities and meanings became a way of keeping his mind focused, active, and alive, particularly in the periods of isolation aimed at breaking him down. And what is most telling is that he never seems to have become tethered to the past through this reflective process. Instead he embraced it as a source of energy for living in the present and projecting ahead to the future he hoped to live for. In taking this approach, he deepened the sense of the context and purpose of his life, which made him doubly formidable as a negotiator and as a leader as he stepped back onto stage as the central actor in the transition to democracy in South Africa.

Then came the key acts. He collaborated with F.W. deKlerk in ending the policies of Apartheid and negotiating the basic terms of the new South Africa. Elected in his nation's first real plebiscite, he served as President, initially leading a unity government that bridged between the old and the new before leading the first fully ANC government. He worked with Desmond Tutu in creating the Truth and Reconciliation Commission, a historic alternative to the stark choice between retribution or blanket amnesty faced by nations emerging from and reckoning with a dark historical episode. In his final legacy as elected leader to his new democracy, he stepped down at the end of his term, setting a norm for its future leaders to live up to.

8.5.1   PERSONAL REFLECTION

Our conviction is that great leaders find a balance between an orientation toward action in the world and an orientation toward reflection. And the good news is that neither isolation nor meditation is necessary to the development of the reflective side of this balance. A leader's reflective capacity can be built and enhanced by individual and interpersonal practice.

Everywhere we look there is reflective practice. Our approach is different in that it centers on a set of specific practices that codify key elements of the process and give structure to what otherwise could become vague musings and revisitations. It marks the difference between learning by chance from experience and being able to trigger a systematic, robust learning experience. One that can be processed either in a few minutes taken at any time, say, as you transition from one thing to another during the day, or as a framework and a point of departure when life affords a longer pause.

At the individual level we have been working for years, in our coaching, with what we call reflective routines, practices that make explicit what many of us do implicitly. The most basic of these is the momentary "pause to reflect" in which the reflector asks a generic question, such as "What stands out for me?" This question can be used to prime a moment of reflection about almost anything.

Often we go a step further, by having our clients work with what we call a reflective routine, a series of seven basic questions that a leader can use to sharpen a moment of pause and reflection, engaging them with the landscapes. It goes as follows:

1. What stands out for me (about this experience, moment, person, group, problem, issue, whatever it may be)?
2. Does anything surprise or puzzle me (that I want to take note of)?
3. What landscape am I most aware of?
4. Are there related issues on this landscape I want to take note of?
5. What happens if I bring another landscape into my perspective?
6. Does this shed new light on what stood out or surprised or puzzled me?
7. Does anything new stand out for me (surprise me and/or puzzle me) now?

One virtue of such a reflective inventory is that it can be used in part or in its entirety depending on the time available. Notice as well that you can use the final question to lead into a second round of reflection. If you have the time to go through several rounds this is a great way to get a sense of the surround, the web of interacting and connected issues we introduced in the landscape chapter. We call this "reflective looping."

Integrating reflective routines or reflective loops into your daily routines, as well as at conscious moments in time (e.g. during or immediately following a *moment of truth*) you will make significant steps forward in understanding yourself and learning from your behaviors.

8.6   Practice 4: Conversational partnerships

Our previous practice, the reflective moment, can be effective as a solitary exercise or as a mutual exercise in which people can often reflect more powerfully than they do by themselves. We want to falsify the myth that reflection is always just about somebody in a personal reverie. We strongly favor and encourage to engage in Conversational Partnerships, simply because dialogue is always more fruitful than monologue.

Our next practice is therefore a set of approaches designed to create the most powerful conversations for change. Up until now much of what we have talked about is the lone explorer struggling against the elements, but guess what? What we have found is that almost every "lone explorer" has been assisted by a dynamic relationship through which he or she has developed their outlook, their vision, and their practice.

Most powerful individuals have a confidant, a conversational partner, a colleague that they can share ideas with and confide their fears, hopes and challenges to. We can call these "conversational partnerships." History is replete with them but we have chosen a few here to disentangle for the purpose of seeing how they work and how they might be used.

8.6.1   MARGARET MEAD AND GREGORY BATESON

In anthropology and human ecology the writers Margaret Mead and Gregory Bateson formed a dialogue that drew great insight into human behavior and the "ecology of the mind."[2] Stemming from their seminal work of visual anthropology in 1942,[3] Gregory Bateson's work spanned nearly four decades across disciplines including cybernetics, ethnology, psychology, biology, sociology, and ecology, but also aesthetics[4] and what he called "an interdisciplinary setting for discussing processes of communication." He was an advanced systems thinker.

Gregory Bateson was an outsider whose intellectual path did not fit neatly within any familiar discipline. He worked with mental patients in Palo Alto and was a participant in formative discussions of cybernetics. For many, this kind of intellectual promiscuity was unsettling. As his daughter Mary Catherine Bateson wrote:

> Each group of specialists was inclined to view work that did not fit into their framework as a diversion – or even as a disloyalty… Experts on whales and dolphins read "Problems in Cetacean and Other Mammalian Communication" and experts on alcoholism read "The Cybernetics of 'Self': A Theory of Alcoholism" to illuminate their own narrowly defined subject matters.[5]

Lacking a clear professional identity, Bateson also lacked a comfortable professional base and a secure income. He was the very opposite of the empire builder who carves out a specialist niche for himself. Despite this he succeeded in having a huge impact, and this would not have been possible without the intellectual and personal support of his wife and colleague, Margaret Mead.

The relationship was clearly reciprocal as we can see in the results of their conversational partnership which produced from her such truly groundbreaking texts as *Coming of Age in Samoa* (1928), *The Changing Culture of an Indian Tribe* (1932), *Male and Female* (1949), and *Culture and Commitment* (1970) amongst many others.

Another extremely influential book by Mead was *Sex and Temperament in Three Primitive Societies* in which she argued that females in the Chambri tribe of Papua New Guinea were dominant. It became "anthropological proof" that male hierarchical dominance was by no means universal.

Though Mead and Bateson are a perfect example of our idea of a conversational partnership as an essential part of a reflective practice – one that in their case tapped into a rich seam of intellectual capital – they are also relevant to the consideration of diversity that we discussed before.

Mead has written that: "If we are to achieve a richer culture, rich in contrasting values we must recognise the whole gamut of human potentialities, and so weave a less arbitrary social fabric, one in which each diverse human gift will find a fitting place." Similarly, Bateson embraces our diversity ethos. As his daughter Mary observes: "He elaborates the notion that, in the world of mental processes, difference is the analog of cause ('it's difference that makes a difference') and argues that embedded and interacting systems have a capacity to select pattern from random elements as happens in evolution."

This shared notion of diversity as a keystone of their thinking was a constant source of inspiration and reflection. Mead was to declare: "Always remember that you are unique, just like everybody else."

Both were in need of support and sustenance, coming under fire for their work in their fields of ecology and anthropology. Mead in particular was accused of having prejudged the situations she pioneered in studying and having imposed her beliefs onto the people she was analyzing.

Neither could have survived – Mead her academic interrogation and Bateson his professional isolation – had it not been for their mutual support. Their conversational partnership was both a source of succor and a platform from which they emerged with renewed vigor, stimulus, and insight.

8.6.2   STEVE JOBS AND STEVE WOZNIAK

A more recent example of a hugely creative partnership that has revolutionized the way we live is that between Steve Jobs and Steve Wozniak who invented the first readymade personal computer. With Wozniak's engineering background and Jobs' marketing instinct, the two started the Apple computer company and revolutionized domestic life and subsequently information storage and consumption.

In transforming the way we live through the revolution that is the home computer, Jobs and Wozniak at Apple Computers offer yet another example of conversational partnership in action. Theirs is a story that seems too far-fetched to be true. It seems like the American dream, a rags-to-riches story of invention and ingenuity.

Jobs and Wozniak came to the conclusion that a completely assembled and inexpensive computer would be popular. They sold some of their prized possessions (Wozniak's HP scientific calculator and Job's Volkswagen van), raised $1300, and assembled the first prototype in bedrooms and garages. The first computer they built was an engineering marvel for its time. In simplicity of use it was years ahead of the Altair 8800, its only competitor which was introduced earlier in 1975. The Altair had no display and no true storage. It received commands via a series of switches (a single program would require thousands of toggles without an error), and its output was presented in the form of flashing lights. The Altair was great for hobbyists, for whom its assembly required nature was actually a feature, but it was not suitable for the wider public. Wozniak's computer, on the other hand, which he named Apple 1, was a fully assembled and functional unit that contained a $25 processor on a single-circuit board. All that was needed was some RAM, a keyboard, and a monitor to make a fully functional microcomputer.

Weeks later, Jobs secured the company's first sale: 50 Apple I computers at $666 each.

In a few short years, Apple was listed in the Fortune 500, becoming the youngest firm on this list. Their conversational partnership seemed destined, as complimentary skills came to the fore when they combined the technical skills for software and hardware (Wozniak) and the design and marketing insights (Jobs) necessary to bring a product to the market. As Wikipedia describes Jobs: "Throughout his career, he has emphasized the importance of design, understanding aesthetics to comprise more than outward appearances alone; his devotion to a refined yet vernacular taste has earned him an equally devoted – some say fanatic – following."

Each came from an immigrant background – Wozniak from a Polish background and Jobs from a Syrian father and American mother who put him up for adoption. While Wozniak provided the detailed technical innovation, Jobs supplied the vision of how these ideas could be applied and the detail of design and usability that would become synonymous with the Macintosh. It was Jobs who would insist on the addition of a dropdown choice of fonts.

For the first time, people could create their own professional quality printed materials. If it was the signal for a deluge of homemade birthday cards, a billion shopping lists and fridge-signs, and death knell for a million forests, it was also the beginnings of an information revolution.

From Bateson and Mead through to Jobs and Wozniak we see powerful examples of individuals leaning on each other in times of stress, drawing wisdom through the strength of two and inspiration through dialogue. If Bateson's wandering generalism was given needed focus by conversation with Margaret Mead, then this was a vital input, and if Wozniak's technical genius was reframed and channeled for public consumption, then all were enriched by the exchange.

History is crowded with dynamic duo-ships, they are everywhere you look. We believe that a conversational partnership is such a powerful means of reflection because it takes you out of yourself and helps you process and comprehend your own actions and challenges and options. The best conversational dialogues are a spur and a foil and a catalyst. By acting together we step away from the isolation that so often prevails. It is a step into the world, for as John Muir wrote:

> Most people are on the world, not in it – have no conscious sympathy or relationship to anything about them – undiffused, separate, and rigidly alone like marbles of polished stone, touching but separate.

8.6.3   INITIATING CONVERSATIONAL PARTNERSHIPS

In our practice we find it useful to initiate peer partnerships to support leaders in reflecting on their immediate leadership challenges and in framing approaches and plans of action for addressing these challenges. This is a form of mutual reflection in which two partners take turns listening to one another and providing feedback by way of questions rather than statements.

We have found it most useful to initiate these conversational partnerships by pairing two leaders of roughly the same organizational level who do not work together directly and ideally are as far remote as possible from each other in an organization and have as little prior knowledge of each other as possible. The partners are provided with a series of written questions and asked to take turns serving as interviewer and subject. The job of the interviewer is to focus on asking and listening with full attention, inviting the subject to reflect on the questions provided. In our classic framework the conversation flows for half-an-hour to forty-five minutes in one direction, after which the partners switch roles and repeat the exercise.

Because most people, even important leaders, do not often experience deep listening for their reflections from their peers, this exercise when properly introduced and debriefed, tends to create a strong bond of mutuality between the partners, usually strong enough that they are able to act as listening partners throughout a series of subsequent exercises in a leadership development program lasting several days. Sometimes these bonds prove strong enough that conversational partnerships initiated in this manner go beyond the duration of the program in which they are initiated.

Developing peer reflection in an organizational context has the potential to provide a complement to the coaching that managers do with the teams they lead. Think of it this way. Within most organizations non-professional coaching is customarily vertically organized up and down a pyramidic structure. Peer reflection offers an alternative that is compatible with such coaching but operates on more of a horizontal basis, permitting leaders several levels down from the top of an organization to have listening partners with whom to try out and refine ideas before they are presented in contexts in which the presenter is likely to be judged. It can also permit the airing and processing of affective material before it spills over into the team context. By having some of the coaching traffic proceed at low risk horizontally, it clears the vertical coaching arteries for their most important functions of performance contracting, delivery, and evaluation.

Of course situations remain, particularly in regard to the most senior leaders and the rising leaders with the highest estimated potential or most serious challenges, in which professional coaching is the wisest course.

8.6.4   COACHING AS CONVERSATIONAL PARTNERSHIP FOR REFLECTIVE PRACTICE

Our approach to leadership coaching begins with the understanding of the coaching relationship as a kind of conversational partnership in which the collaboration focuses on the *individual landscape* of the one being coached. In this context, coaching is less an instrumental exercise aimed at specified targets such as job performance goals and more of an exploration of ways in which the wider life context can be developed so that multiple levels of enhanced performance can be achieved, sustained, and generalized.

Several elements combine to accomplish this. First, a comfortable level of mutuality needs to be found in which the coach and client are working more like the examples of conversational partners we met in the preceding pages. In this case the attitude of coach and client, side by side, reflecting together on the client's life and work is what stands out. In this sense the conversational partnership becomes an undergirding and formative platform for reflective practice.

Second, our approach brings key elements of this book together as an integrated practice. We see the coaching relationship as a generator of reflective practice in which the partner being coached is supported in reflecting on how goals they are working on relate to multiple landscapes of their work and lives. We help them to clarify, explore, and renovate their underlying assumptions about the situations they face and to assess their performance. In the light of feedback, achievements and setbacks – including those highlighted in previous coaching conversations and those which are newly emerging – are reconnected with the *enduring commitments* and deep intents of the person being coached. They then set the course for their *immediate intent* and design the immediate scripts and longer-term strategies with which they will approach their intended goals.

Third, our coaching conversations focus on the landscape of the individual where our guided reflections explore and clarify how various dimensions of the landscape are impacting each other while working to develop a more robust integration of the whole territory. Our generic map of the individual landscape relates the following four dimensions in an integrated frame (as mentioned in our examples at practice 2: *inquiry mapping*):

1. The first dimension is the domain of **Meaning and Purpose**. What anchors meaning in your life? How do you make meaning and find purpose in your work and your life? What commitments have endured for you over the long run? How are these commitments expressed as deep intents in this chapter of your life? How do you deal with your successes? How do you step up to challenges? How do you cope with

obstacles, disappointments, and setbacks? Because leadership typically requires sacrifices, what tradeoffs make sense in your life and how do you justify them to yourself?

This dimension of meaning and purpose connects directly with our equanimity profile. The strength of an individual's capacity for constructing meaning stems from the alertness of their *eye for possibility* and is grounded in their *enduring commitments* and deep intents. The capacity to reframe your approach or to shift to another perspective requires a lively sensitivity to possible alternative frameworks of meaning. The step from recognizing diversity to connecting with diversity in ways that expand your boundaries and welcome the experiences of others requires constructing new meaning. It entails reconsidering and possibly *reframing* how you see the world. The *eye for possibility* links directly to the ability to face new situations, and recovering yourself when thrown off your balance relates to the anchoring meanings in your life and to your capacity to reframe meaning in the face of challenge.

2. The second dimension is **The Project**. It is the domain of work and performance, the leadership context, focusing on the individual's immediate and longer-term leadership goals and challenges. This is where the coaching conversational partnership usually starts and where it focuses most often. After initial issues have been sorted out, the priority turns to exploring connections and possible disconnects between the domains of the project and of meaning and purpose. This permits us to draw the aspects of equanimity into the practice field of the project. It is also where we focus on the remaining aspect of equanimity, "exercising and projecting presence." It is also about how you show up as a leader, which is foremost a function of how well you exercise *presence*. This dimension is also the portal into other leadership landscapes identified in Chapter 2 such as the team, the organization, the industry, and the society as well as to the exploration and mapping a wide range of alternative landscapes which may be identified in the course of the coaching conversation.

3. We term the third dimension **Life Contours and Balances**. This domain integrates the narrative of the leader's whole life. We work with it from the perspective of figure and ground, almost like a computer desktop except that the foreground image is multidimensional and all of the background images (the folders on the desktop) are all in sight and configured in a surround. Each image, representing an aspect of life, can be brought into the foreground individually or in combinations for the purpose of seeing interdependencies and contradictions, while maintaining the sense of the whole. The images feature familiar titles including, starting toward

the center of the screen and radiating outward in concentric circles life history, career history, the realm of domestic life and relationships, the leader's interests and avocations, friendships, voluntary associations, along with issues of heath and well being, ultimately all of the attributes that together form the ecology of each client's life and identity.

4. Our fourth dimension is the **Materials**: the domain of financial assets, obligations (debts, mortgages, insurance), and compensation as well as the realm of possessions and philanthropies. It also includes planning for the future, including retirement and the education of children. While we recommend a professional financial advisor for direct work on many of these issues, our approach focuses on how these issues relate to performance, well being and development of the leader in general and, in particular, to the other three domains, meaning and purpose, the project, and life contours and balances. We refer to the fourth domain as the material side and we focus on several key concerns. Are the necessary means available to support your leadership projects? What about your life beyond your work? What tradeoffs are you making between the material side and the other three domains? Are income and aspirations proportional? If not, what is a workable strategy for bridging the gap?

8.7 Practice 5: FutureFacts

Our final practice is one that specifically focuses on the ability to Reframe and sharpen the *eye for possibility*, usually on the landscapes of Macro Business, Industry and Markets, and Organization. It is the practice named FutureFacts,[6] a powerful methodology to embrace the future, enter into team dialogues about what is coming at the horizon, anticipate changes, and stimulate entrepreneurship and innovation by "seeing things early."

FutureFacts is a variation to the widely published form of Scenario Planning. It is a process analogous with an oil refinery. It takes crude sludgy stuff and refines it till it becomes a product that can lubricate the parts of a highly sophisticated piece of machinery. The sludgy stuff is the "guestimates," random unconventional ideas, and projections gathered together in a set of "FutureFacts." A FutureFact is an imaginary future event that brings a specific changing reality to the surface.

The FutureFacts process consists of three phases:

1. Creating FutureFacts
2. Storyboarding futures
3. Drawing implications.

8.7.1   PHASE 1: CREATING FUTUREFACTS

Creating FutureFacts is a process of creativity and imagination. By abiding to a set of well-defined creation rules, a rich set of inspiring, innovative, challenging, provoking, and even threatening ideas are gathered and written up as a FutureFact. The creation process is as important as working with the materials, as it forces one to entertain stretching and unconventional changing realities that could possibly become realities and change our frame in the next five to seven years. This is where the first learning takes place, as the otherwise hidden reality of broadly described changes, is brought to the surface by plausible, real-life future "news facts" that would change our realities. In consulting projects we run, this is often done during a phase of preparation with the core client team. Ideally, however, this is an on-going process adopted by key thought leaders in the organization and can be a very powerful mechanism to embrace the future, with the opportunities and threats it contains, on a continuous, interactive, and inspiring way. Some companies we work with have allocated a physical space where these FutureFacts are posted and can be read by others. This way they serve as constant reminders and sources of inspiration to the company as a whole, sharpening the collective *eye for possibility*.

The creation process therefore serves multiple purposes. From an organizational learning perspective, it is a powerful way of embracing the future, "creating a memory of the future,"[7] as veteran scenario planner Arie de Geus calls Scenario Planning. It also serves as an early warning detection system – typically, the exact imagined events do not literally come true, but as the future unfolds, new information that relates to the "guestimates" is mentally processed in a different way and patterns that evolve are earlier detected and comprehended than they are by your competitors. One could therefore say that creating FutureFacts is a *reflective moment* on the future. It is Practice 3 applied to the future.

8.7.2   PHASE 2: STORYBOARDING FUTURES

Periodically, the process of contemplating future events is paused by creating Storyboards of the Future. This process, based on lessons drawn from the art of building powerful stories, bundles and integrates different perspectives represented by the set of FutureFacts to form appealing, plausible, and defendable stories. Multiple stories are the result of this process, typically 3 to 6, where each story is tested on plausibility and defendability.

The art of Storyboarding Futures is again built around the ability to engage with the future in an imaginative way. By using tested artistic storyboarding techniques, powerful stories emerge that can be visualized and "lived" powerfully, before they possibly unfold. As multiple stories get developed, we avoid the pitfall of narrowing ourselves to a one tunnel vision view on the future. The richness of the stories help us in developing acceptance and mental agility for the different ways in which uncertainties can play out.

8.7.3   PHASE 3: DRAWING IMPLICATIONS

In order to bridge creativity to the real world, where the results of our imagination can be used in a powerful way to create or test strategies, stimulate entrepreneurship and innovation, and develop strategic options, a third step is entered: drawing implications. Assuming for each world that it will happen, we derive the implications. From the collective learning, we first can filter out those things that turn out to be generic. Also, by combining outcomes, we are generally able to uncover creative, integrated approaches to strategic challenges or opportunities. This plays into the desire to make well-informed choices and ensures for robust decision making.

The FutureFacts process can be applied on a project basis – for example to deal with a particular challenge – or on an on-going basis. We have been involved in efforts that involved just the 15 business and thought leaders of the company, to efforts in which we engaged over 3000 people in an in-depth exercise to uncover the future, using FutureFacts. On a business level, such a "business-creative" process is a vital element in progressing integrative thinking into being a dynamic strategic worldview.

The FutureFacts process particularly works on the equanimity dimensions of *reframing* and *eye for possibility*, generally on the Industry and Markets and Macro-business perspectives. It is often used in teams, but can as easily be applied by individuals that desire to develop a better understanding of the dynamics of the world they are possibly going to live in. We advocate this process as it approaches strategy from an outside-in direction, instead of an inside-out direction often witnessed in practice.

What we mean by this is the following. The FutureFacts methodology looks explicitly at the world outside the organization first, as it provides the pivotal context of the world the organization will live in. In our landscape terminology, these are the landscapes of the Industry and Markets and Macro-business perspective. It is in that part of the future reality where customer preferences shift, where technological innovations take place, where regulators change the rules of the game, where competitors challenge conventions, where economic forces drive new value and focus, and so on. So it is against that background that the organization must discuss their current and desired position, and initiate the actions to reach that position.

Even though this sounds blatantly straightforward, in most businesses we witness that strategic discussions and decision making generally do not seriously and structurally visit these "outer" landscapes, but are boxed in by the confinements of the own organization. The Organization Landscape becomes the start and endpoint of the strategic exploration. The unit of research is foremost the organization, its problems and limitations, its drivers, its edges, its growth paths, its ambitions, its stakes, and so on. And with clarity provided around these themes, the outside world is visited to find the trends that can provide support for these arguments. It is the inside-out approach we resist, as it leads to little entrepreneurial and innovative thinking. It also carries with it a high degree of risk in creating strategies that are not aligned with the (long-term) future. We therefore advocate the outside-in approach, which pays its first stop in creating an understanding of the world and the future we will live in, independent from our own organization. It is the starting point of innovation and of the greatest entrepreneurs, so why should it not be the starting point of the strategic process. Methodologies such as FutureFacts are among the best suitable, creative approaches to work with the future in such a "business-creative" way.

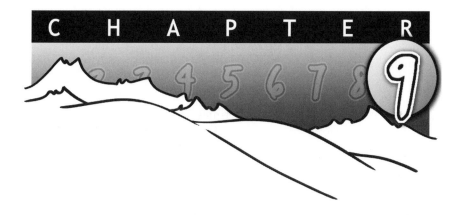

Classical Illustration

> *I may say that this is the greatest factor – the way in which the expedition is equipped – the way in which every difficulty is foreseen, and precautions taken for meeting or avoiding it. Victory awaits him who has everything in order – luck, people call it. Defeat is certain for him who has neglected to take the necessary precautions in time; this is called bad luck.*
>
> The South Pole, by Roald Amundsen

As we reach the end of our journey with you, it is time to reflect on our endeavor together. We challenged you with two key perspectives to understand and improve leadership – your leadership. We elaborated in detail on how we see *leadership landscapes* and the *equanimity shift*. Then, we took you through several real-life *moments of truth*, where leadership is called for and demonstrated how our "tool base" comes to service in those moments. Lastly, we have provided you with a range of practices to ensure yourself, as well as your team, and to sharpen your leadership edges by applying specific practical practices.

137

We have thereby aimed at providing you with a start to end journey to work toward mastery. Throughout we have provided "snippets" of examples from business leaders, world leaders, thought leaders as well as "ordinary" leaders doing extraordinary things. We would like to close our journey however with a journey of a very different kind. It illustrates not only how in great leadership our perspectives come to the surface, but also that what we advocate is for all times. And was already understood and practiced by a great discoverer, and great leader, Roald Amundsen.

Roald Amundsen (1872–1928) was a Norwegian explorer whose leadership and strategy exemplify all of the elements we espouse in *leadership landscapes.* He led the Antarctic expedition of 1910–1912, which was the first to reach the South Pole. Before that he was the first to traverse the Northwest Passage across Greenland, bridging the Atlantic and Pacific Oceans. This was a long cherished dream of maritime seafarers and the location of many tragically failed ventures.

Amundsen's success in the face of overwhelming conditions is a worthy model for any examination of leadership qualities. It also serves as an illustration of how Amundsen's supreme qualities of equanimity helped him achieve these seemingly impossible journeys.

9.1 The Northwest Passage

The Northwest Passage is a sea route from the Atlantic to the Pacific through the Arctic archipelago of Canada. The potential for a lucrative trade route was one of the incentives for travel and exploration of this region and a matter of considerable national competition.

Efforts to find a navigable summer route through the thawed ice floes was attempted by a series of expeditions, none succeeding over a 500-year-period from 1539, when Hernán Cortés commissioned Francisco de Ulloa to search for a route, to the early 20th Century. In 1578, the Yorkshireman Martin Frobisher tried three times to find a passage and failed on each attempt, although he succeeded in charting some of the area.

John Davis, an Elizabethan navigator who later "discovered" the Falkland Islands, tried on several occasions to chart a route. In 1585, he started on his first northwestern expedition. He began by striking out for the icebound east shore of Greenland, which he followed south to Cape Farewell before turning north once more up the west Greenland banks some way. Finding the sea free from ice, he shaped a course for China by the northwest. Though he pushed some way up Cumberland Sound, he turned back by the end of August. He tried again in 1586 and 1587.

In 1609, John Hudson sailed up the river that now bears his name and explored the Canadian Arctic searching in vain for a passage to the Pacific.

The first half of the 19th Century saw a series of attempts – all of which failed. In 1818, John Ross, a Scottish explorer, received the command of an Arctic expedition organized by the British Admiralty, the first of a new series of attempts to conquer the passage. This entailed going around the extreme northeast coast of America and sailing to the Bering Strait. Whilst Ross was to fail on this and two subsequent trips, one almost ending in tragedy for all aboard in 1832, he was successful in bringing back accounts of the currents, tides, and state of the ice as well as an extensive collection of specimens he found on the way. Several subsequent efforts followed throughout the 19th century – each effort was thwarted by sickness, extreme cold and storms, changing ice floes, or other disasters. Yet, each expedition brought back improved charting of the seas and open terrain, essential information for a region that physically changed from season to season and that held few reliable points of reference.

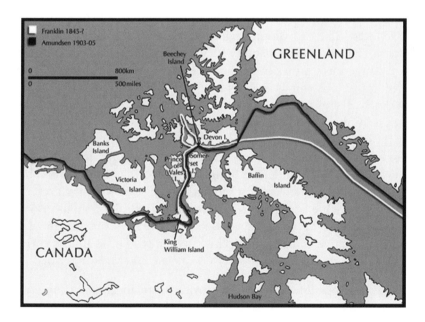

As failure piled on failure, governments threw more and more resources at the expeditions, desperate for the national glory and potentially lucrative trade routes that a successful search could yield.

9.2 The man who ate his boots

The two expeditions we will look at are the John Franklin expedition of 1845 and the Amundsen expedition of 1903–1906. Despite the fact that half a century sits between their attempts, it is worth comparing the radically different approaches used by the two expedition leaders.

In 1845, Franklin left Britain equipped with two schooners and 129 men in search of the fabled Northwest Passage. He was a highly experienced officer who had served at the Battle of Trafalgar and by this time a veteran Arctic explorer. Franklin first traveled to the Arctic in 1818 as a lieutenant under the command of John Ross. He was to lead his own expedition the following year. On a disastrous overland party into the Northwest Territories of Canada along the Coppermine River in 1819–1821, Franklin lost 11 of the 20 men in his group. Supply routes were cut and relations with the local indigenous people deteriorated. Most died outright of starvation, but there was also at least one murder and even suggestions of cannibalism. The survivors were forced to eat lichen and even attempted to eat their own leather boots, which gained Franklin the nickname of "the man who ate his boots."

The ordeal had been horrific but little questioning of Franklin's leadership resulted. The expedition's failure crudely exposed Franklin's weaknesses as an explorer: an inability to adapt to unexpected circumstances and a dangerously inflexible adherence to his instructions and prearranged plans. But this was a rigidly hierarchical Victorian society and Franklin had shown great personal courage, an attribute prized above strategic thinking and innovation at the time.

In the intervening years, he led expeditions up the Mackenzie River and to the Beaufort Sea as well as serving a doomed spell as Governor of Tanzania.

But in 1845 Franklin left in high confidence. The ships he had been given were sturdy, and were stocked with three years worth of preserved food supplies. One of the consequences of Franklin's previous doomed mission was that he would never again rely on a supply chain of fur traders and native Indian allies. This time he would be almost entirely self-sufficient. As the *Dictionary of Canadian Biography* described:

> Everything possible was done to provide for the health and comfort of the officers and men: heating was supplied by steam-boilers serving a network of pipes; each ship carried huge quantities of the latest patent preserved foods, china, cut glass, and silverware; and large libraries and other educational aids were available. Just the clothing might have seemed inadequate – standard naval cloth supplemented only by underwear and wolf-skin blankets – but then the expedition was not expected to linger in the Arctic.

The expedition ended in complete failure and the death of all. They got lost, illness struck the crews, and eventually they became stuck on the ice and slowly died off.

Of a further 30 expeditions to find Franklin's men during the period 1847–1859, just four managed to piece together the basic facts of Franklin's last years.

Historians have now grown to the consensus that what really finished the expedition was its maps. They were a mixture of accurately recorded detail, blank spaces, and pure conjecture.

King William Island was believed to be part of the mainland, which we now know it is not. Based on this wrong assumption, Franklin concluded that the passage was closed off to the east and sailed west. As the ships became trapped in the ice, the men onboard had no option but to wait for the summer and pray that the ice thawed before it grew thick enough to burst through the ships' hulls.

As there had not been any news from Franklin three years after the mission had set out, driven on by Franklin's widow the British Admiralty mounted a massive search costing an estimated £30 million and risking more lives. With national pride at stake, they financed three teams of rescuers, but nothing was found.

Then out of the blue, in 1854, the explorer John Rae reported meeting Inuit people who told him they had found the remains of white men who had died of starvation in their camp. They also described how the men had been driven to cannibalism – a report which caused mayhem in Victorian Britain and was roundly denounced as a lie. A final expedition in 1857 failed to find the men or their ships, but did find a document that shed some light on their fate.

It stated that ten months after the men became trapped in the ice, Franklin and several other senior men had died. The document, left on a cairn on King William Island also stated that the 105 men left, decided to abandon the icebound ships and trek across the ice floes to America. They never made it – dragging boats weighed down with Bibles, portraits of the Queen, shelter tents, and firewood – they were prey to exhaustion, extreme cold, starvation, and scurvy.

9.3   Franklin's perspective

Essential in our perspective toward leadership is the capacity to identify parts and the connections among them as coherent patterns. It is also essential to see oneself as part of those patterns and simultaneously to step outside and reflect on them. Hence our descriptions of the navigation across the landscapes, the equanimity attributes of *reframing* and *recovery*.

It is clear that Franklin was unable to do this. He was entirely bound by the worldview he inhabited. Each time the British Admiralty were beaten by a failed expedition, they threw more of their culture and more of their might at the problem. More men, bigger ships. An imperial approach was simply defeated by the forces of the Arctic environment. In one sense, this is not Franklin's fault. He was tied to a naval command which itself was representative of the British state at the height of its imperial ambition. In this era and culture, the Inuit people were simple savages and to learn from or interact with them would have been pointless.

Also, Franklin did not succeed in another key aspect of leadership, which is to take a relational worldview that sees things as fluid and ever shifting – and needing an appropriately flexible response. His world was governed by immutable truths and absolute rules. A chain of command, an unquestioning hierarchy, a God and a Queen Ruling with Divine Right, and laws of racial and cultural superiority. Science and scientific enquiry were often used to perpetuate the status quo rather than as pure enquiry. The results were emphatic: death from starvation, cannibalism, and abject failure.

Of the dozens of expeditions that went out to attempt to traverse the Northwest Passage (several involving Franklin himself), little was learned. Repeatedly, missions would go out into one of the most hostile terrains imaginable and come back empty handed. Expedition after expedition, there seemed to be little progressive or tactical changes. Yes, each hopeful group would return with a little bit more of the map filled in, but little was truly learned.

The attempt by Western European explorers to find the route through the Northwest Passage is a brilliant, shining example of people locked in a single paradigm. They were unable to see the context of their actions, unable to critically evaluate their work, unquestioning of its value, and doomed to repeat failed actions over and over again to considerable expense and loss of life.

In a business context you could compare this process with being stuck in an unacknowledged paradigm, perhaps in a rapidly shifting marketplace. This is about noticing assumptions and noticing the perspectives we are stuck in. What is embedded in your operational assumptions that is different from your competitors? What is the wider context in which your business operates?

9.4   Amundsen's breakthrough

Roald Amundsen was the fourth son in the family. His mother tried to keep him away from the sea pressuring him instead to become a doctor.

This was a promise that Amundsen kept until his mother died when he was 21. He was born in Borge in the southeast of Norway and very early became fascinated with polar exploration. In fact, he was enthralled by reports of the doomed Franklin expedition and Fridtjof Nansen's crossing of Greenland in 1888.

An early experience as a second mate in a botched Belgian Arctic expedition of 1897 where a poorly prepared crew was forced to spend a winter west of the Antarctic Peninsula was highly influential. Amundsen began to reflect on the whole of the situation and began to understand the key dimensions involved.[1] Let us look first at how his approach led him to be the first European after a 500-year-long struggle to find a route through the Northwest Passage and then how he became the first man to the South Pole.

For one man to have conquered the Northwest Passage, the North Magnetic Pole, and the South Pole is almost beyond imagination; yet Roald Amundsen accomplished all three in less than ten years. The vessel Amundsen selected for the voyage was the *Gjøa* – a 47-ton, 70-foot sloop which set out from Oslo in June 1903. The *Gjøa* crossed the North Atlantic and then hugged the west coast of Greenland before crossing to the northern end of Baffin Island. The voyage continued as the Norwegian party started to make its way through the labyrinth of islands off Canada's northwest coast. They faced constant hazards of icebergs, storms, and blizzards but eventually found refuge in a natural harbor on an island, northwest of Hudson Bay.

For two years the expedition remained at the port that the men named Gjøahavn. There they built observatories, equipping them with high precision instruments. The studies they undertook not only established the position of the magnetic North Pole, but also included observations of such precision that they provided experts on polar magnetism with sufficient work to last them for 20 years.

Crucially, Amundsen also learned from the local Netsilik people how to drive dog teams, what clothes to wear, and how to catch food in what might appear an Arctic desert. He studied their customs, storing it all in his retentive memory for later use in polar regions. He had realized the terrible irony that Franklin's men had starved in a land where there was a rich supply of food (there were caribou, seal, birds, and fish in plenty) and alliances where Franklin saw only hostility.

One of Amundsen's many innovations was to hug the coastline – having figured that ice is less thick close in to the coast. He not only took his own route rather than follow in others' footsteps, but he also followed that route in his own style. Bit by bit they crept along the coast making gradual but definite headway week after week. Their small vessel could go where the larger ships had been unable to, and they were able to fish and live off the land as they went.

It is said that at times the water was so shallow in the channel that the vessel had only one inch of water beneath its keel. As the *Gjøa* moved slowly along its course, Amundsen and his crew realized that they would soon be in waters that were known and charted by navigators moving eastward from Alaska. After three weeks the expedition sighted a whaling ship out of San Francisco. The *Gjøa* had successfully navigated the Northwest Passage, the first vessel ever to do so.

The vessel froze in the ice and Amundsen set off in October with dog teams, travellng almost 500 miles across the ice to Eagle City in Alaska, where he telegraphed the outside world with his achievement. He had been preparing for two-and-a-half years for an assault which took barely three months.

His new found fame was a spur, and he was able to quickly find support for his real aim –the North Pole. Amundsen borrowed the ship *Fram* ("forward") from Fridtjof Nansen – who had used the boat drifting with the ice from Siberia between 1893 and1896. Nansen agreed and an expedition was put in place. However just as everything came into view, the sudden news arrived that an American explorer, Robert Peary, had reached the North Pole. In an instant Amundsen changed his plans and headed for the South Pole instead. It was widely known that the English explorer Robert Falcon Scott was attempting – for the second time – to reach the South Pole.

In January 1911, the *Fram* reached the Bay of Whales, a site the Norwegians had identified in advance that they knew was 60 miles closer to the Pole than Scott's base. Amundsen placed way markers along the first part of the route that would also serve as provisions. All was dependent on attention to detail and innovation in logistics. In preparation over the winter, Amundsen's teammate Olav Bjaaland reduced the weight of his sledges from 165 pounds to just 48. Amundsen, after an initial false start reduced his team by one, whilst Scott, who died in his failed effort to reach the Pole, had a late addition to his team. Also crucially, while Scott's team used tractors and ponies, Amundsen used 100 Greenland huskies, which he had shipped specially. They arrived at the edge of Polar Plateau on November 21 after making good progress. In a typical piece of ruthless ingenuity, shortly afterwards, 24 of the dogs were killed and fed to the remaining pack. On December 13, 1911, a team of five Norwegians arrived at the Pole, 35 days ahead of Scott's team.

In examining Amundsen's approach to planning and leading the expeditions, we can see many of the key elements of Integrative Thinking exhibited. He developed a deep understanding of the key dimensions of the challenges he faced: at the widest scale to change the relationship with nature and at the most precise detail despite operating in the most extreme weather conditions.[2] He also understood the relationship between his tools and his team, his project and his wider goals, his short-term tactics and his long-term strategy (being to return to the North Pole).

There are a number of other elements worth appraising.

▶ **He had precise attention to detail as well as having a constant in his mind of the whole surround.** After a fallout with one member of the team just before the assault on the South Pole he dropped him later on and made the group smaller and tighter. He could do this because all the men were trained in all the necessary skills. Amundsen himself wrote in his autobiography:

> How did I happen to become an explorer? It did not just happen, for my career has been a steady progress toward a definite goal since I was 15 years of age. Whatever I have accomplished in exploration has been the result of lifelong planning, painstaking preparation, and the hardest of conscientious work.[3]

▶ **He changed the rules of the game.** Where John Franklin took 129 men, Amundsen took just six across the Northwest Passage and just eight to the South Pole, of which only five made the final part of the journey. Where Franklin's approach opted for "safety in numbers," Amundsen opted to pick out a select team with all the qualities and skills he required: navigation skills, endurance, seamanship, bravery, and strength. Skills in cross-country skiing and dog handling were learnt by all, offering maximum flexibility. Further, Amundsen realized that the potential for disharmony amongst 100 plus men isolated for months or years is very high. A small group is easier to lead and meld into a tight team with strong goals.

▶ **He reframed his view of the problem.** Whilst Scott followed the route of his predecessor Ernest Shackleton, Amundsen forged a completely new route which proved to be the more accessible.

▶ **He designed and obtained all the necessary tools for his expeditions.** His ship for the successful assault on the Northwest Passage – the tiny *Gjøa* – was only 70 ft. It was cheap and all he could afford, but it had been used by Norwegian sealers operating in Northern Scandinavia. In modern parlance it was "fit for purpose." His ship for the Antarctic expedition, the *Fram* has been described as possibly "the strongest wooden boat ever built." It was specially designed for Fridtjof Nansen's 1893 Arctic expedition by the renowned boatbuilder Colin Archer. The ship was designed to float across the Arctic when it froze. The rudder and propeller were designed to retract into the ship if necessary. It had a thick hull of greenheart wood to withstand the ice and, crucially, it was almost without a keel. This virtually flat-bottomed boat would allow it to navigate very close in to the shore where the ice was less thick or non-existent. He understood – at the widest landscape possible – the need for cultural attunement to the people who lived and had lived for millennia in Arctic conditions. In other words, he entered into a dialogue. Amundsen spent almost two years in dialogue with the Netsilik people. He respected them and their ways and delayed when members of his team wanted to press on. This was a deep engagement with this culture over several seasons living amongst them and fully inhabiting their world. It was not a casual copying or "lifting" of a few key skills but an immersion in the Inuit ways.

▶ **He changed the mindset.** Amundsen clearly reframed the entire terms of the challenge. While Franklin and to an extent Scott relished the rigors of self-sacrifice, Amundsen, who had grown up in semi-Arctic conditions was quoted as saying: "There is no virtue in suffering, and the real hero avoids suffering." The polar historian Roland Hunter has remarked:

> The English hero, particularly Franklin, is the romantic hero, and he is always associated with suffering. But the kind of hero that Nansen was, the kind of hero that Amundsen aspired to be, and the kind of heroism that is embedded in the Scandinavian psyche, is the diametric opposite. The hero is the survivor. It's the Homeric hero, in the wonderful opening words of the Odyssey: "Tell me, o muse, of the man of many wiles.[4]

▶ **He motivated and inspired those around him by leading from example.** When he had changed plans to travel to the South Pole, instead he traveled to Madeira before letting the crew know of the change. Every member of the crew stood by him and accepted the new plan unquestioningly, which suggests a great trust and confidence in his leadership.

▶ **He took risks and was able to be flexible to rapidly changing conditions.** As soon as he heard that he had been beaten to the North Pole, he quickly changed plans completely, turning instead to the South.

▶ **He persevered.** When he first set off for the Northwest Passage he was severely in debt. If the expedition had not succeeded, he would have been bankrupt. Describing the scene Amundsen wrote:

> Finally, on the morning of June 16, 1903, I was confronted with a supreme crisis. The most important of my creditors angrily demanded payment within 24 hours, with the threat that he would libel my vessel

and cause my arrest for fraud. The ruin of my years of work seemed imminent. I grew desperate and I resolved upon a desperate expedient. I summoned my six carefully chosen companions, explained my predicament, and asked if they would cooperate with me in my strategy. They enthusiastically agreed. Therefore, at midnight on June 16th, in the midst of a perfect deluge of rain, we seven conspirators made our way to the wharf where the *Gjøa* was tied, went aboard, cast off the hawsers, and turned southward toward the Skagger Rack and the North Sea.

This is a man who displays great patience, fortitude and immaculately detailed planning, but if the moment comes, he is hardly ponderous.

▶ **He had detailed knowledge of the dynamics and dimensions of the challenge.** One of the key problems was disunity amongst the expedition force. In his autobiography he writes:

By this time I had read all the books on the subject I could lay my hands on, and I had been struck by one fatal weakness common to many of the preceding Arctic expeditions. This was that the commanders of these expeditions had not always been ships' captains. They had almost invariably relied for the navigation of their vessels upon the services of experienced skippers. ... Always two factions developed – one comprising the commander and the scientific staff, the other comprising the captain and the crew. I was resolved, therefore, that I should never lead an expedition until I was prepared to remedy this defect.

Amundsen would not be curtailed by having a separate owner of the ship, a state sponsor or a split command. He was beholden to no-one and entirely in charge of his expeditions.

▶ **He exhibited great qualities of equanimity.** Roland Hunter, the polar historian, is quite clear that one of the distinguishing features of the English and Norwegian attempts was their contrasting approaches. While Franklin was the romantic hero struggling to overcome nature, Amundsen was the diligent practitioner working with nature. This more positive approach, Hunter argues was the hallmark of the Norwegian outlook: "Norwegian explorers are always looking for the silver lining, even if it is the sun shining for a nanosecond in a blizzard."

The lessons learned between Franklin's and Amundsen's time have been long debated and the battle between Scott and the Norwegian for the South Pole has been the subject of drama, film, book, and endless scholarly discussion. On the face of it, Amundsen succeeded because he saw the whole picture. Rather than attempting to conquer nature, he resolved to live in his new habitat instead of trying to survive "above" it. The lessons gained in the first expedition were carried forward into future challenges: his husky trip over the last hurdle in the Northwest paid off well in Antarctica. His ability to commune with the Inuit gave him survival skills of a higher order than Scott's team possessed. His use of skis was the result of long-term strategy working with Norwegian seal hunters from whom he also learnt key skills of arctic navigation and seamanship.

He was able to see emergent possibilities when others would see only closing doors of opportunity. The way he was able to overcome the apparent duality between native Inuit technology and culture with his own culture's more "advanced" skills and techniques was a key breakthrough. For example, he learnt how to make clothing out of caribou hides but also waited and waited near the North Pole taking magnetic readings that helped him keep a precise chart of his location.

Across all of our Landscapes, Amundsen's leadership excels. His individual qualities of leading the team, engaging stakeholders, concentrating and appreciating his calling, and raising the necessary resources were all met. If integrative thought is the capacity to identify parts and the connections among them as coherent patterns, to see oneself as part of those patterns, and simultaneously to step outside and reflect on them, his leadership is an exemplar of our practices.

N O T E S

Preface

1   James Botkin, Mahdi Elmandjra, and Mircea Malitza, *No Limits to Learning,* London: Pergamon Press, 1980.

1   Introduction

1   John O'Neil, *Paradox of Success,* New York: Tarcher, February 1994.

2   Leadership Landscapes

1   Peter Senge, *The Fifth Discipline: The Art and Practice of the Learning Organization*, New York: Currency, 1994.
2   For example: Charles Hampden-Turner and Fons Trompenaars, *Riding the Waves of Culture: Understanding Diversity in Global Business*, New York: McGraw-Hill, 1998; Gregory Bateson and Rodney E. Donaldson, *Sacred Unity – Further Steps to an Ecology of Mind*, San Francisco: Harper, 1991.
3   William James, *On a Certain Blindness in Human Beings*, New York: Areprint Service, 1923.
4   See Kenneth E. Boulding, *A Primer in Social Dynamics: History as Dialectics and Development*, New York: Free Press, 1970; Richard Rorty, *Philosophy as Cultural Politics*, Cambridge: Cambridge University Press, 2007.
5   Jim Collins, *Good to Great: Why Some Companies Make the Leap ... and Others Don't*, New York: HarperCollins, 2001.

3   The Equanimity Shift to Dynamic Balance

1   Laurent A. Daloz, Cheryl H. Keen, James P. Keen, and Sharon Daloz Parks, *Common Fire: Leading Lives of Commitment in a Complex World*, Boston: Beacon Press, 1997.
2   http://en.wikipedia.org/wiki/Equanimity, accessed on April 15, 2007.

3 For more background to the concept of equanimity we articulate here see: Alexander W. Astin and James P. Keen, "Equanimity and Spirituality," *Religion and Education* (Spring 2006), Vol. 32, 2, pp. 36–49.
4 Thomas L. Friedman, *The World Is Flat: A Brief History of the Twenty-First Century*, New York: Farrar, Straus and Giroux, 2005.
5 *The Independent* on Sunday, September 4, 2005.
6 http://www.netimpact.org/, accessed on May 22, 2007.
7 www.forbes.com, accessed on April 18, 2007, "The World's Billionaires," Louisa Kroll and Allison Fies, editors. March 2007.
8 *Business Week*, November 14, 2005.
9 *Economist*, 2005, eighth position of Most Admired Global Leaders.
10 *Financial Times*, 28th position of World's Most Respected Business Leaders.
11 Viktor Frankl, *Man's Search for Meaning*, Boston: Beacon Press, 1959.
12 Laurent A. Daloz, Cheryl H. Keen, James P. Keen, and Sharon Daloz Parks, *Common Fire: Leading Lives of Commitment in a Complex World*, Boston: Beacon Press, 1997.
13 http://www.momentis.uk.com, accessed on March 4, 2007.
14 http://www.davidpearlgroup.com, accessed on July 9, 2007.
15 Michael Useem, *The Leadership Moment: Nine True Stories of Triumph and Disaster and Their Lessons for Us All*, New York: Three Rivers Press, 1999.

4   Leadership Seeing

1 http://www.future-facts.com, accessed on July 9, 2007.
2 Viktor Frankl, *Man's Search for Meaning*, Boston: Beacon Press, 1959, p. 86.
3 Ibid. p.133.
4 For two books that long ago inspired our thinking on reframing, see James Adams, *Conceptual Blockbusting*, Cambridge, MA: Perseus Books, 1974, and Roger Fisher and William Ury, *Getting to Yes*, Boston, MA: Houghton Mifflin, 1981.
5 W. Chan Kim and Renee Mauborgne, *Blue Ocean Strategy*, Watertown, MA: Harvard Business School Press, 2005.
6 Dove site at www.campaignforrealbeauty.com, accessed on July 9, 2007.
7 Dove used StrategyOne and MORI International as well as the American Council of Research Organisations (ACRO) and enlisted academics such as Dr Nancy Etcoff from Harvard University and Dr Susie Orbach from the London School of Economics.
8 For an excellent analysis of the generic pattern of post-conventional reframing that characterizes Silvia Lagnado's work, see Mary Belenky, Blythe Clinchy, Nancy Goldberger and Jill Tarule, *Women's Ways of Knowing*. New York: Basic Books, 1986.
9 Reflection from Tom Cummings.

10 Ken Wilber, *A Theory of Everything*, Boston, MA: Shambhala, 2001, p. 55.
11 Nansen was a legendary figure in polar exploration. He and his crew had spent three years between 1893 and 1896, drifting with the ice from Siberia towards the North Pole.
12 In fact they did – setting up a series of presentations and lectures in Harlem and recruiting young people from inner cities for future Antarctic expeditions and projects.
13 *The Economist*, August 5, 2006.
14 http://en.wikipedia.org/wiki/Crowdsourcing, accessed on July 12, 2007.

5 Leadership Being

1 Michael Useem, *The Leadership Moment: Nine True Stories of Triumph and Disaster and Their Lessons for Us All*, New York: Three Rivers Press, 1999.
2 Laurent A. Daloz, Cheryl H. Keen, James P. Keen, and Sharon Daloz Parks, *Common Fire: Leading Lives of Commitment in a Complex World*, Boston: Beacon Press, 1997.
3 Jim Collins, *Good to Great: Why Some Companies Make the Leap ... and Others Don't*, New York: HarperCollins, 2001.
4 Nelson Mandela, *Long Walk to Freedom*, Boston, MA: Little, Brown and Company, 1994, pp. 21–22.
5 Ibid. pp. 364–365.
6 Ibid. p. 368.

6 Leadership Doing

1 Michael Useem, *The Leadership Moment: Nine True Stories of Triumph and Disaster and Their Lessons for Us All*, New York: Three Rivers Press, 1999.
2 Graham Allison, *The Essence of Decision: Explaining the Cuban Missile Crisis*, Little, Brown and Company, 1971.
3 Jerry B. Harvey, *The Abilene Paradox and Other Meditations on Management*, Lanham, MD: Lexington Books, 1988.
4 Fons Trompenaars, *Did the Pedestrian Die: Insights from the World's Greatest Culture Guru*, Oxford: Capstone, 2003.

7 Moments of Truth

1 http://en.wikipedia.org/wiki/Rich Hall, accessed on July 14, 2007.
2 Rich Hall, *Sniglets (Snig'lit : Any Word That Doesn't Appear in the Dictionary, But Should)*, New York: Collier Books, 1984.

3   John Adair, *Effective Strategic Leadership: An Essential Guide to Success by the World's Great Leaders*, London: Pan Books, 2003.
4   Jim Collins, *Good to Great: Why Some Companies Make the Leap ... and Others Don't*, New York: HarperCollins, 2001.
5   Cartier-Bresson, *The Defining Moment*.
6   Michael Moore, *The Official Fahrenheit 9/11 Reader*, New York: Simon & Schuster, 2004.

8   Toward Mastery

1   John O'Neil, Leadership Aikido: *6 Business Practices That Can Turn Your Life Around*, New York: Three Rivers Press, 1999.
2   Gregory Bateson, *Steps to an Ecology of Mind*, New York: Ballantine, 1972, and *Mind and Nature: A Necessary Unity*, New York: Dutton, 1979.
3   Gregory Bateson and Margaret Mead, *Balinese Character: A Photographic Analysis*, New York: New York Academy of Sciences, 1942.
4   See for example Gregory Bateson and Mary Catherine Bateson, *Angels Fear: Towards an Epistemology of the Sacred*, New York: Macmillan, 1987.
5   Foreword to the new University of Chicago Edition of *Steps to an Ecology of Mind*, 2000.
6   http://www.future-facts.com, accessed on July 18, 2007.
7   Arie de Geus, *The Living Company*, Watertown, MA: Harvard Business School Press, 2002.

9   Classical Illustration

1   For example see Roald Amundsen, *The South Pole: An Account of the Norwegian Antarctic Expedition in the "Fram," 1910–1912*, Northampton, MA: Interlink Publishing Group.
2   In the five months Amundsen and his team were on Antarctica temperatures varied between −58° and −74°F.

INDEX